# How To
# SAVE YOUR STUFF
## From A Disaster

## Complete instructions on how to protect and save your family history, heirlooms and collectibles.

Scott M. Haskins

Preservation Help Publications
Santa Barbara, California
1996

This book is printed on acid-free buffered paper.

ISBN: 0.9649647-0-8

The information in this book is furnished for informational use only, is subject to change without notice, and should not be construed as a commitment by Preservation Help Publications or Scott M. Haskins. Preservation Help Publication and Scott M. Haskins assumes no responsiblility for any errors or inaccuracies that may appear in this book.

All brand or product names are trademarks or registered trademarks of their respective holders.

Printed in the United States of America

Published by:

Preservation Help Publications
P.O. Box 1206
Santa Barbara, CA 93102
(805) 899-9226
(800) 833-9226


Publishing Date: October 1996

# Testimonials

### *"How To Save Your Stuff From A Disaster"*

*"This book should be stored in a safe place along with the other vital necessities in case of a disaster in the home.  As a self-help book it is the ultimate manual to have at hand when the dispiriting and depressing task of "cleaning up" begins.*

*The instructions are easy to follow, the materials listed are inexpensive and easy to find.  This is a must-have book for anyone who prizes the family's photos, papers, paintings, books, collectibles and other easily damaged items, even without a home disaster.*

*There are also many terrific and inexpensive suggestions for caring and protecting precious and irreplaceable family items in the home on a day-to-day basis.  The suggestions on the organization of family papers, school and family photographs, genealogical documents and records are excellent.  This book provides clear solutions for a number of problems that families face in storing, sorting and preserving items for the future."*

**Juanita Thinnes, Past President**
**Friends of the Historic Mission Inn**
**Genealogist, Riverside, CA**

*"Francis Bacon (1561 - 1626) said, 'Some books are to be tasted, others to be swallowed and some few to be chewed and digested.'  This volume surely belongs in the latter category.  This is a book that would make Lewis Carroll's Alice very happy:  "Lots of pictures and conversations.' ...a jolly good read!"*

**Kenneth Winslow, V.P.**
**Butterfield and Butterfield Auction**
**House**

# Testimonials cont...

*Thank goodness for "How to Save Your Stuff!" For nearly twenty years I have felt so very helpless when someone would call me after a disaster. When I think about the need for Scott's book, many sad stories come to mind. I remember the woman who had placed a box full of family heirlooms of Lemoge China on the top shelf of her closet in order to protect them. When the Northridge Earthquake (Los Angeles, 1994) hit, the box fell to the floor and the entire set was lost.*

*I had the opportunity to work with Scott on educating the public when the Northridge Earthquake occurred. Scott wrote a booklet entitled, "How to Care for your Valued Family Possessions Before, During and After a Disaster." Several hundred thousand copies were distributed in the L.A. area.*

*As a manufacturer and distributer of conservation products for the professional conservation field, I have had the privilege of watching this brilliant field of art caretaking grow, and I have been fortunate enough to have a first-row seat to such conservation projects as the Portland Vase restoration and the Statue of Liberty. My friends and colleagues are people dedicated to the preservation of art and artifacts. Scott is one of these people.*

*There are two things that can destroy your own treasured family items: one is not knowing what to do (this book fixes that), and the other is procrastination. As you read Scott's book, walk through your home and ask yourself what you can do to protect those items most important to you. Whether your "stuff" is old and comes to you from other generations or is new and is "just" your kids schoolwork, all of these items tell your story and hopefully can live on from one generation to another.*

*"How To Save Your Stuff From A Disaster" translates the technical world of professional art conservation to you. Scott gives you simple, easy to follow instructions (its the only book of its kind!) and empowers you to take proper action. No longer must your stuff be at the mercy of the next disaster!*

**Dorothy B. Adams, President**
**Conservation Materials, Ltd.**

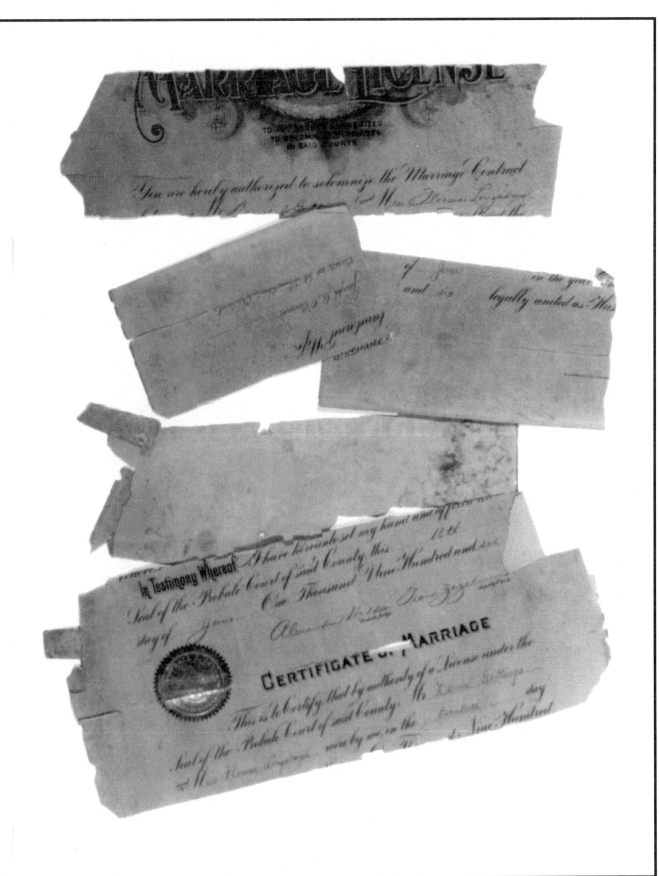

# Contents

# Credits

*Editor:* Preservation Help Publications

*Illustrations:* Joan Haskins
*Photography:* Scott M. Haskins
*Desktop Publishing:* Image Quest Design
*Cover Design:* Steve Cerocke/Scott Haskins
*Other Contributors:* Dorothy B. Adams

# Acknowledgments

I acknowledge the great patience  my kids have had with me and thank
them for their encouragement and prayers.
I love them with all my heart.

Thanks also for the comments and counsel from professional associates
and friends who have been very encouraging and helpful.

And, most of all, I thank my Heavenly Father for the opportunities to
grow and for his support.

# Preface

Have you ever lost a possession that was dear to you in an earthquake?  Porcelains that broke, a book that was ruined by water or photos that stuck together in a pile, perhaps rugs or pictures that were burned or blown away.  What are you afraid of losing in the next big one?

I've been involved in six "major" disasters:  three earthquakes (Sylmar '71, Whittier '89 and Northridge '94), two fires (Santa Barbara '90 and Oakland '93) and one flood (Santa Barbara '95).  Although people lost homes, cars, toys, etc. the items for which I have heard the most crying was for the things that made up a people's family histories.  "Stuff" that may not have had much monetary value... things that cannot be replaced with insurance money.

With all the insurance, laws, programs, books and disaster preparedness drills we go through to protect ourselves and our homes, you never get any help knowing what to do about the memorabilia that you hold dear.  So here it is!  This book is the easy to read version of the information published in professional conservation publications by practicing conservators whose job it is to help clean up after messes that Mother Nature makes... or that your grandkids make.

Although I've tried to make this book enjoyable to read *(This is a book that would make Lewis Carroll's Alice very happy: 'Lots of pictures and conversations.' ... a jolly good read!" says Mr. Kenneth Winslow, V.P. of Butterfield and Butterfield Auction House, San Francisco),*  I don't expect you to read the book cover to cover.  Each chapter deals with whatever you may have to work on.  Keep it handy as a reference book to be consulted as you organize your boxes of stuff, put together scrapbooks or reorganize your garage.

This is  not a book for professionals.  When possible, I have suggested using materials that are easy to find (local store, warehouse supply or hardware store).  But some things that you will want to buy need to be purchased from a specialized supplier.  Their names and numbers are in the back of each chapter.  None of the suppliers have paid me to be mentioned in this book.  They are genuine referrals based on my knowledge of their good service and/or quality supplies.  A good idea would be to call each of the (800) telephone numbers and request a free catalog.  We do this in my college class and we use the catalogs as our text books.  They are very informative and you will learn a lot by browsing through them.  Besides showing you their items for sale, they often make good suggestions for working techniques.

DO NOT START BY ORGANIZING EVERYTHING NOW.  Protect and preserve (notice I didn't say 'restore') the 5 items most important to you... start there.  One bite at a time.  I guarantee that the organization (to be done later) of the "whole pile" will go much smoother and safer if you will follow this important suggestion.

There is almost a spiritual identity that people feel for the items that tell their family's story. I remember when, on TV, Joan Rivers was talking to Dorothy Adams of Conservation Materials Ltd. about Quake Wax. Among the hype, hustle, lights and make up (she wore a lot!... can we talk!?) there was a moment when Joan softened and became emotional when she realized that had she used this product, she would have saved a dear ceramic keepsake from the Northridge Earthquake. It was a gift from her husband who had recently passed away. She became really quite emotional about an item that was worth very little money.

Maybe you want to put your children's school momentos in order or you may be the caretaker of the family photos, letters, certificates and portraits: stuff that may have been unceremoniously dropped on you after Auntie's passing on. Whether you are a collector or you're old enough to be an antique yourself, there are lots of hands on, how to instructions in this book that will help you to protect and preserve your family's history, memorabilia and collectibles. God bless you for taking your project to heart. Preserving your family's history will benefit more people than just you.

I would very much like to hear from you! Please write me about your successes and problems. Let me know of your experiences and stories. Write me at: pH Publications, P. O. Box 1206, Santa Barbara, CA 93102 or E-Mail: artdoc@earthlink.net

Best wishes,

Scott Haskins

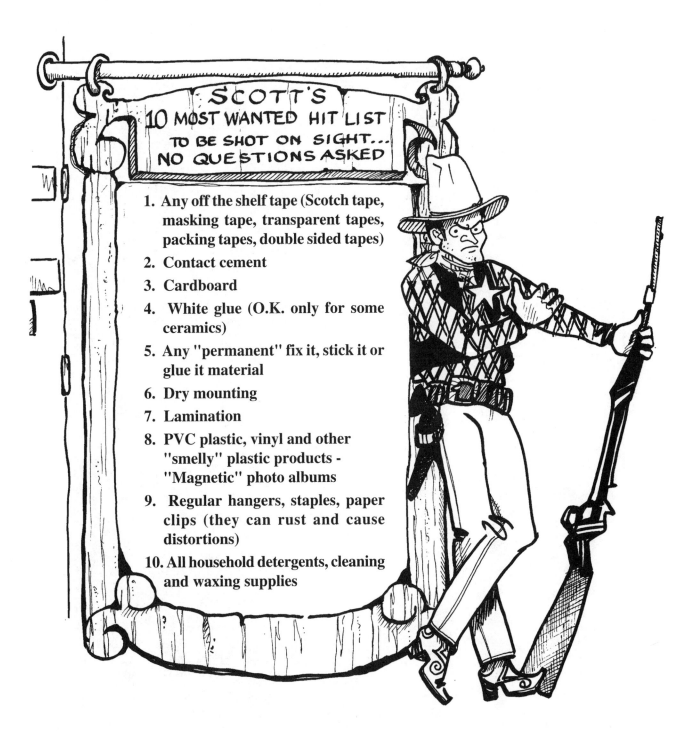

SCOTT'S
10 MOST WANTED HIT LIST
TO BE SHOT ON SIGHT...
NO QUESTIONS ASKED

1. **Any off the shelf tape (Scotch tape, masking tape, transparent tapes, packing tapes, double sided tapes)**

2. **Contact cement**

3. **Cardboard**

4. **White glue (O.K. only for some ceramics)**

5. **Any "permanent" fix it, stick it or glue it material**

6. **Dry mounting**

7. **Lamination**

8. **PVC plastic, vinyl and other "smelly" plastic products - "Magnetic" photo albums**

9. **Regular hangers, staples, paper clips (they can rust and cause distortions)**

10. **All household detergents, cleaning and waxing supplies**

# CHAPTER 1

# Photographs and Negatives

## *Before A Disaster Occurs:*

We all have piles of photographs lying around in drawers, boxes, whatever. I'm sure you would like to organize them into cute books, but the discussion on putting together an archival photo album will have to be put off for another time. The first step is to make some progress in their protection. I would like this to not be laborious or difficult.

Read the section "Paper Items" for additional information.

**In a nutshell, what we want to accomplish first off is:**

♦ Separate them so they don't damage each other.

♦ Arrange them so they are easier to browse through.

♦ Protect them in case of disaster.

All three of these very important needs will be fulfilled by taking a couple of simple steps. Here are the ways you go about getting the job done:

The best way to make sure the photos don't stick to each other is to find a way to store them so they don't lie around in a pile touching each other. Try one of the following two suggestions:

♦ Buy three-hole-punch archival plastic pages for storage of the photos and negatives and then, once filled, put your pages in any school notebook with a plastic cover (colored cloth covers could bleed colors on your photos if gotten wet) and/or...

♦ Use an archival "shoe box" type approach with archival separating papers (interleaving sheets). I guess it depends on your personality as to which one you choose. They both work.

I have spoken with some people that like the shoe box approach because they store easy. I personally like the plastic page approach, so that's the one I'm going to tell you about. You can look through the supplier catalogs to see what suggestions they may have.

The correct plastic used for the pages should be polyester, polypropylene or polyethylene. Besides being good for photos, these materials won't transfer the wording off of your photocopies onto the plastic. Bad materials to be avoided are vinyl, polyvinylchloride (PVC) or anything that smells weird or strong. The offgassing vapors will ruin the colors of new photos and accelerate the aging of old ones.

Don't use the magnetic page photo albums either. The plastic on the front is always bad and the stickum on the back will eventually hold the photo so tight that you won't be able to get them out safely. I've seen people rip their photos trying to get them out of old magnetic albums. The pages also yellow badly and look bad. The appeal of the "magic page" is short-lived, believe me.

The pages that I recommend are clear plastic and you slide the photo in from the top or side. The pages come divided into sections for numerous photos and you can put the photos in back to back, thereby getting two photos in every slot. If you do this however, you can't read anything you've written on the back.

You can pay full price ($ .50 each) for the right kind of pages at your local photo specialty store or you can buy them bulk wholesale through a mail order company like

Vue All (see "Suppliers of Preservation Materials" list) for as little as $.22 per page (100 per package). I have also bought them every once in awhile at the large warehouses like Price/Costco. Inquire around. You may be able to get them at stores like Fedco or Walmart.

Each page comes divided into sections the size of individual photos. The 3" x 5" and 4" x 6" sizes are the most common sizes for color prints. You can buy all 4" x 6" pocket pages if you don't mind the 3" x 5" photos sliding around a little. If the prints look like they could slide out of the pocket, try stapling or taping the pocket shut with a special double sided tape, polyester 3M No. 415. See "Suppliers of Preservation Materials." You will also need storage pages for strips of negatives (labeling with subject and date is especially important). You may also need 8" x 10" pages. They make all kinds.

In order to quickly get through the task of putting all your prints, negatives and slides into the pockets on these pages, I don't recommend trying to completely organize the photos or even looking through them to reminisce on the great vacations or B- day parties. The very most you should do is try to get, maybe, all one child's photos into the same book or all of the same vacation photos together. Just do a general categorizing and get them into the page protectors. You could write on the top of each page a note about the identification of the photos, and if you can, I suggest you include the year the photos were taken.

Also, at this point, don't worry about the rips, stains, folds, etc. The information on how to do these preservation minded tasks is in the up-and-coming book (send in the enclosed post paid card to get on the mailing list). Remember, just get the job done as quickly and as thoroughly as possible.

The first step: Get the photos into page/photo protectors and put the pages into a notebook. Organize and label later.

3M No. 415 (sounds like a secret agent's number) is a double sided adhesive tape used only for adhering Mylar sheets together. It is used by the Library of Congress and professional conservators.

I found this acid free Mylar photo album at Price Costco for under $10.00.

As an alternative to using the plastic page protectors, I have also found and used already-made photo albums from large warehouse type stores. The albums are advertised as having pages made of acid-free materials and photo-safe plastics (no PVC). Providing you can believe what they tell you, these albums are probably OK to use. If you would like to be really sure, check the album for the company's #800 phone number and ask them to confirm that everything is on the up and up.

If you have large historical photos or some of odd sizes (like the 10" x 48" panorama photos) you will need to buy a special "holder" just for that item. Consider some of the archival boxes or specialty envelopes and enclosures in the catalogs listed at the end of the chapter or look through the plastic container section of your supermarket. These containers are made of polyethylene or polypropylene (acceptable archival materials).

Once you have page protectors full of photos, you do not need to get a fancy archival notebook. Any school notebook with a plastic cover (colored cloth covers could bleed colors on your photos if gotten wet) will do for now. The photos are safe in their pages and even though the notebook is not archival quality, the photos and negatives will be safe. Be sure to label what is in the notebook.

By taking these simple steps to separate and safeguard your photos (which could be done while watching TV), you will have made sure that they will not stick together if the weather gets hot and humid or if the photos get wet. You will have also protected them from getting fingerprints, bent edges and they won't get scratched up (like the ones in your drawers). These efforts will help you to feel much better about their preservation. You may even sleep better (no need to send me a fee for therapy).

Also of great benefit now, is when you go looking for a photo, all you need to do is pull out the notebook from the bookshelf or storage box and leaf through the pages. When you are finally ready to make the creative archival photo album for each child, you will already have a good start.

If you are going to put the photo albums into storage (because you won't be getting them out very often to look through them), I suggest you get a large plastic (polyethylene) container (like Rubbermaid or Tupperware). They can be sealed to keep out bugs, varmints and water. Also, these heavy-duty containers will fare better in an earthquake. I suggest not putting them in the attic or barn (it is too hot or too cold) or basement (water gathers in low places). Keep them in a cool dry place like under a bed or behind a sofa.

Please note also that in the event of a disaster which involves water, you will have the photos stored in a clean manner. Cardboard boxes and the like not only soak up water, but the cardboard itself will bleed off impurities when wet and the yellowing will be carried by the water to stain everything thing else around. Your foresight will keep this from happening.

## *After A Disaster Occurs:*

- ◆ DON'T STACK WET PHOTOS INTO PILES!

- ◆ DON'T TOUCH THE SURFACE OF THE WET PHOTO!

- ◆ DON'T LET ANYTHING TOUCH THE WET PHOTO SURFACE!

- ◆ DON'T PULL STUCK PHOTOS APART!

The following is a list of types of photography and what should be done if they get wet. After this list is a general explanation on how to go about their salvage and preservation (see Section "What to do and how to do it"):

Here is a list of the different types of photography and what should be done if they get wet.

## *Modern photography:*

**This is your priority list, as far as which type of photography needs to be saved first, if you have to choose what to save from a disaster:**

1. Color prints, then

2. Black and white prints, then

3. Slides (transparencies) and then

4. Negatives

This list is based on the fact that color prints will be damaged by water the fastest and so on... then, of course, your priority may be to save the photos of the kids first... After the emergency situation has passed and you have made sure that everyone is safe and as soon as you have gathered your wits about you, your immediate decision is needed for the salvation of your family's photos:

♦ Dry them out or...

♦ Freeze them (so you can work on them later) within 72 hours or...

♦ Keep them in clean cold water (change the water daily) until you can do something.

It is imperative that the impurities are washed out and that the film does not stick to itself (which it will do if it starts to dry out). If you have more afflicted photos than you can take care of, I recommended that after putting the film into a basin filled with cold temperature (distilled) water, that the help of a photo lab be sought out. Once the film has been washed and stabilized and dried, it is important to store it properly, even temporarily, such as in a sandwich bag or other archival material.

Motion pictures should be rewashed by an experienced film processing lab within 72 hours. Until you can get the wet film to them, fill the film cases with clean cold water or put into a basin of water (change the water daily) so they won't dry out and stick to each other. Once the film has been washed, stabilized and dried, it is important to store it properly, even temporarily, such as in a sandwich bag or one of many other archival boxes from the suppliers at the end of the book.

### *Microfilm rolls:*

It is imperative that the impurities are washed out and that the film does not stick to itself. Because of the sheer volume of material to be handled, it is recommended that after putting the film into a basin filled with cold temperature (distilled) water that the services of a photo lab be sought out within 72 hours. Do not remove the film rolls from their boxes. Instead try holding the cartons together with string or a loose rubber band. Once the film has been washed, stabilized and dried, it is important to store it properly, even temporarily, such as in a sandwich bag or other archival material.

### *Old black and white prints on paper:*

Keep in clean cold water (so they don't start to dry out and stick together) until you can do something. If they are going to sit in a basin of water for a couple of days, be sure to change the water daily. The photos must be dried separately within 72 hours. If you cannot properly dry them or get them to a processing lab, see the following section on how to freeze photography.

If you have other types of old photos but don't know what kind they are, call a photographic conservator immediately. Do not pass "GO." Do not collect $200.00 If you know what you have, the following list should help put the fear of God in you. They are all super sensitive and the success rate for recovery is low (in this case an ounce of prevention is worth more than a pound of treatment):

Tintypes, ambrotypes, pannotypes and collodion negatives are a first priority item! They need to be dried immediately, face up. Do not put these types of photos in the freezer and do not put them in a basin of water as this will destroy the emulsion. Be prepared that the success rate for recovery is low, but this may depend on your care. Be careful when handling the delicate glass supports.

Daguerrotypes need to be dried immediately, face up. Don't put them in water and don't freeze them.

Nitrates with soluble emulsions need to be put in the freezer immediately. Try freeze drying. Very touchy, be careful when handling.

Let me emphasize again how important it is to get the advice of a professional conservator who specializes in photography as soon as possible. Please refer to the section at the end of the book on "How to Find a Conservator."

### *What to do and how to do it:*

Old paper backed photographs (vs. plastic coated new photo prints) may be yellow and brittle. Because of these deterioration problems, handling your old vintage photos on paper while wet, compounds your problems and could result in your causing more damage when handling them than occurred as a result of the disaster which you recently experienced.

No matter what kind of photographs you have, if they get wet, they are your No. 1 priority. Red alert. You must act now, while they are wet if you want to increase your chances of salvaging your photos. This should be done within 72 hours. Don't let them dry out (if they are in a pile).

If you have a large quantity of wet modern photographs or if you have motion picture film on rolls, then you may not have any choice but to go to a photo lab for help. If your photographs are very old or antique, it would be best to consult a conservator who is specialized in photographic preservation and understands the dangers and can deal with the problems of deterioration of old photographs in addition to the damage.

Remember, once dried, the photographs, especially color photographs, which are securely stuck together, may have a very low percentage chance of separation without damage. Keep them wet till they can be worked on.

---

*How do you know if the photo is plastic coated? Wipe a damp finger across the back of the photo. If it absorbs the water, it is paper. Also, paper is easy to write on, the plastic is hard to write on (the pencil or ink doesn't stick too well).*

*I found a plastic container (made of the "right material") full of color prints on Kodak paper at a friend's house not long ago. It was one of the "piles" on her "To Do" list. They were all stuck together into one solid pile.*

*So be forewarned: even if you have the photos in a good container... even if they are kept in a place as dry as a bedroom... photos stacked in a pile can stick together.*

*So what happened to them? They sat around for a long time, then she threw them away... when it came time to do something about them, she didn't even ask me how to TRY to get them apart!*

The worst situation in which you may find your photography is if they are stuck together in a pile. Photographs and negatives have a surface coating (an emulsion) which, upon getting wet and then drying, may have adhered itself to the print next to it. DO NOT TRY TO PULL THEM APART! You need to be very careful when handling wet and damaged photos as they will be especially fragile.

If your photos are ripped, stained, dirty, bent or wavy, there's no hurry. They won't get worse if you take care of them. Your only priority in an emergency situation is to keep things from getting worse and to preserve that which could be further damaged.

If you find a pile of color or black and white photographs or negatives stuck together, the first thing that should be done is to put them into a large basin of clean cool water. DO NOT TRY TO PULL THEM APART! It is possible that the photos emulsion will swell in the water and release the photo attached to it. You may have to leave it in the water for 24 hours. Make sure the water stays clean.

If your photographs are stuck together because they have gotten wet, and if they are still wet or damp, it is best to get them into clean cool water as soon as possible. Do not let the wet or stuck together photographs dry out, if at all possible.

### *How to Freeze Photography*

**If you have a large amount of wet photography that you cannot deal with immediately (within 72 hours):**

1. Remove them from the basin of water.

2. Rinse off dirt, mud, and scum under gentle running water.

3. Do not try and separate any photos stuck together.

4. Separate with wax paper all individual photos or groups of photos.

*Don't let photos sit in dirty water.*

5. Put them into ziplock freezer bags.

6. Put them in the freezer (yes, even your one at home will do if you have room, but don't stack the steaks on top!) and freeze them within 72 hours. Call a local meat processor, ice cream company or other commercial freezer for help with a lot of items.

By either freezing or getting your photographs into a basin of cool or room temperature water immediately, you will avoid the prolonged humid conditions that are conducive to mold and mildew.

### Unfreezing Your Photographs

**If you have frozen your photographs, the best way to save them is:**

♦ Ask around town for freeze drying services. This is often the best technique for drying which results in less damage. There are problems with freeze drying photos, however, so consult a professional photo conservator.

♦ Take them to a photo processing lab (not a "1-hour" place)

**If you have to do it yourself, get some consultation from a professional photo conservator:**

♦ Only defrost as much stuff as you can easily handle (space for washing, drying etc.).

♦ Put the frozen photos into a basin of cool water and let them defrost at room temperature (kind of like your frozen turkey).

♦ Let the photos separate themselves over a couple days (change the water so it stays clean).

♦ Any photos you try to detach will probably have part of the photograph pulled off.

♦ Once separated, rinse and let them air dry as described later in this chapter.

## *Mold*

Mold is one of the more severe problems you will have to deal with if your photos get wet and stay damp. That is why it is so important to take action as soon as possible after the unfortunate disaster. Once your photos get it, it will be hard to get rid of.

*Do not try to rub mold off of wet photographs.*

**Let me summarize what I have already written with a list of what you can do to minimize mold problems:**

- Set up fans to circulate the air, no heat.

- Dry the items within 72 hours, no direct sun or heaters in a closed area or...

- Freeze all items that cannot be dried.

- If you have to let something sit in a tub of water, change the water every 24 hours.

**If your photographs have already been afflicted by mold or mildew:**

- Get them dry as soon as possible (moldy items are high priority!). This stuff grows fast!

- Protect yourself with a face mask with a carbon filter (mold spores are very small and may penetrate regular dust masks). Some people are allergic to mold.

- Outside, away from other papers, photos, etc., remove the surface mold with a very soft, clean brush. Don't let the mold dust get on anything else or later, when the humidity rises, the mold spores that have settled will grow again.

- If there is a residue on the surface of the photo, take a cotton swab and wipe the surface with iso-propyl alcohol. This should remove the mold and may even kill some of it.

The more severe the problem the more you will need professional help. The older the photo, the more urgently you will need a specialized professional.

### *Mud*

Photographs covered in mud also need to be cleaned off (see next paragraph) and dried within 72 hours, otherwise interleaf the photos with wax paper and freeze them. Drying can be done by circulating cool air (with a fan) through the room. If you turn on a heater (in a attempt to dry things out more quickly), you will only cause the humidity to rise and mold will grow more vigorously. Expect some mold growth anyway.

Malibu, California: Mud Slides. The photo remained stained even after the mud was carefully picked off. This photo was hand colored and the colors came off with water!

If you have a fresh (it just happened and is still wet) mud problem, rinse off the photos using a gentle flow of cool water or by gently swishing it around in a basin (kind of like panning for gold). DO NOT RUB ON THE PHOTO. If you can, get the mud off while it is wet. There is more likelihood of staining if the mud dries.

For dried mud, put the photo(s) in a basin of clean water. After letting it sit for an hour, gently rinse clean. DO NOT RUB ON THE PHOTO.

CAUTION: Old, hand tinted, colored photos are often colored with paints that dissolve in water. If you rinse them, you will wash off the color. Getting some advice from a professional photo conservator won't cost you anything. Do it.

**There are two alternatives to handling a wet or muddy stack of photos yourself.**

♦ Take your pile of modern photos to a professional photo lab (do not take your negatives and photographs to a fast photo type store). If possible, you should take your photographs to the photo lab with the photos in a basin of water. The best way to transport the wet stuff may be to line a pail with a clean trash bag liner then fill the pail with cool water and photos. Let the technician separate and dry the photographs and negatives. They have the equipment and know how to separate, rewash with proper chemicals and dry your photographs and negatives so that your chances of success in saving them are greater. Do not take old photographs to these guys.

♦ A professional photographic conservator will not only be well prepared to assist in general salvage, but will be particularly skilled with the old vintage photography, unlike the photo lab.

If it is not possible for you to take your photography to an expert, see the next paragraph for drying instructions. After drying, protect them with proper storage.

### *Drying Wet Photography*

**Do not under any circumstances use:**

- ♦ Bleaches
- ♦ Detergents
- ♦ Fungicides
- ♦ Disinfectants
- ♦ Staples or paper clips

If you are going to attempt to separate your modern photography by yourself, it is best to let the photographs separate themselves over a twenty-four hour period in the basin of water. You can let them sit longer (in fact you may have to) but be sure you change the water every 24 hours. When handling the wet photographs, do not rub, mush, or caress the surface, as this will damage the emulsion and the image. If possible, use a pair of blunt tweezers and hold the photograph by the edges. Once the photographs have separated, it would be best to rinse or dip the

What a disaster: During a recent trip my kids informed me that a gallon of water had emptied into my briefcase! Photos, a book, letters, bills...all got wet. I put the book under weight to dry. The photos separated easily enough while they were still wet. Then I laid them out flat on paper towels to dry. Photos that turned odd colors when wet turned back to normal when dry. Yea! Everything turned out all right (except I haven't got the stain out of my leather bag yet).

The original was cracked, broken and had missing pieces.

The "restoration" did not restore the original photo. Instead, a copy was touched up.

photographs in a basin of clean, room temperature distilled water. Do not let photos sit in dirty water.

Photographs on plastic coated paper can be hung, on a string which is stretched across the room, with clothespins but don't do this with old photos on paper. The old brittle deteriorated paper will fall apart. If you do not have a lot of photographs, they can also be dried face-up on a towel in the open air but be careful where you set them out. Gusts of wind or a wandering dog could really make a mess.

♦ Cloth towels will wick away any water and should be lint-free, if possible.

♦ You could also use unprinted newsprint paper or butcher paper, with less success.

♦ Avoid placing wet photos on your old newspaper, colored paper or other easy to find papers. Inks can smear, dyes and colors can run, and acid deterioration products could be absorbed by your paper backed photography when wet.

**You may accelerate the drying with a blow dryer:**

1. Don't blow the item off the counter; use low blowing pressure.

2. Hold the hair dryer about 20" away. You can set the heat setting on hot, but...

3. Do not get the photograph hot.

At this point, your photograph is detached and impurities may have been washed away. You have saved your photograph but after drying, you may have ended up with a warped photo. This may be one of the drawbacks of doing the work yourself instead of having a professional help you. The photographs, once dried, can then be placed in individual protective sleeves. Besides using the photo sleeves or other enclosures and archival envelopes to protect the photos mentioned in the preceding section, you could also use sandwich bags from your supermarket (they are pretty flimsy though) and then put them in a protective box (see references for catalogs at end of book for archival boxes or use a Tupperware or Rubbermaid type box). Make sure your photographs are completely dry before placing them in any holders.

If you have photographs that have been ripped, scratched or otherwise damaged, don't despair. You may find that for your most important photographs, professional re-touchers will be able to do a very satisfactory job helping you restore the image (they will touch up a reproduction of your photograph). For the restoration and conservation of original photography, please consult a professional photographic conservator.

### *Photo Albums:*

If your photographs are in a photographic album and the album has been destroyed by water, try to remove the photographs from the album and discard the album. This may be easier said than done. There are a lot of things that can make the salvage process difficult: inks that run, glue that won't release, paper colors that run. You will need a lot of patience and the advice of a professional photo conservator wouldn't hurt. If pages are stuck to the photographs, place the pages of the photo album and the photographs together into the basin of water, as explained earlier in the chapter. As soon as you can remove the photos, pull the pages out of the wash water and then change the water. Do not let photos sit in dirty water.

**If there is writing in the photo album that needs to be recorded, preserved, or remembered, take every handling precaution possible to not have the paper pages fall apart when wet:**

- ◆ Use wet strength paper towels to support pages from below while moving them.

- ◆ While trying to remove photos, use little spatulas or a small knife to gently detach hard to get apart areas... you'll need some finesse... patience.... don't just rip it apart.

- If you want to run water over the pages to remove gunk deposits, don't let the tap run water directly on the page. It will tear it into little pieces.

- Do not try to "dry the page off" with a towel, Let it air dry (or help it with a hair dryer if you want) face up on cookie racks or on paper toweling (which should be changed as it gets soaked).

Once the photographs are removed, the pages can be air dried and then photocopied to preserve the information for transcribing at a later date into a new photo album.

## *Conclusion*

You need to remember something: once you have salvaged from water, cleaned off, and dried your family history photographs, they will not be in a perfect, restored condition. You will have done your best but the casualties will be high. That's the nature of the beast, photography. Earthquake damage will be much easier to deal with.

**The important thing is to remember your priorities:**

- What is most important to you?

- Can you get a copy of something lost or damaged from someone else?

My suggestion is to try and salvage everything from the disaster, but when it comes time to clean up and recuperate, save your most important things first, if you can.

What's better, if the major disaster hasn't happened to you yet, read the section on "Before a Disaster Occurs" one more time.

Courtesy Gaylord Bros.

Movie film must be stored in clean acid free boxes to minimize scratching.

# *Supply Locator: Photographs & Negatives*

| <u>Supply</u> | <u>Number or Other Resource</u> |
|---|---|
| | (Numbers correspond to vendor number on next page.) |
| Bags, freezer zip lock | 6, 7, 8, Supermarket |
| Bags, sandwich | 8, Supermarket |
| Bags, trash | Supermarket |
| Containers, plastic (Tupperware or Rubbermaid) | Supermarket, Drug store, Warehouse store, |
| Plastic page protectors | 1, 2, 3, 5, 6, 7, 8 |
| Paper, butcher | 3, Paper supply |
| Paper, unprinted newsprint | 3, 7, Paper supply |
| Photo albums | 1, 3, 6, 7, 8, 10, Stationary store, Warehouse store |
| Racks, cookie | Supermarket |
| Spatulas, small | 1, 3, 7, 8, Art store |
| Tape, double sided #415 | 1, 2, 3, 6, 7, 8 |
| Towels, cloth, lint free | 1, 2, 3, 7, 8, Paint store |
| Towels, paper, wet strength | Supermarket |
| Tweezers, blunt | 1, 3, 7, 8, Drug store |
| Water, distilled | Supermarket |

# SUPPLIERS OF PRESERVATION MATERIALS

**When you cannot find what you need at the local store, here is a list of suppliers who will have the hard to find stuff. Call the #800 and ask for a free catalog. They are usually very informative. Also, the lists of materials mentioned from each chapter have numbers that match with the suppliers on this page, so you know who sells what.**

**1.** Conservation Materials Ltd.
Box 2884, Sparks, NV  89431
Phone Toll Free (800) 733-5283
Phone (702) 331-0582
Fax (702) 331-0588
General preservation supplies.  Has Collector Care Kits, scrapbooks and photo albums.

**2.** United Mfrs. Supplies, Inc.
80 Gordon Drive, Syosset, NY 11791
Phone Toll Free  (800) 645-7260
Fax:  (516) 496-7968
Hardware

**3.** Gaylord Archival Preservation & Conservation Supplies and Equipment
Box 4901, Syracuse, NY 13221
Phone Toll Free (800) 448-6160
Fax:  (800) 272-3412
General preservation supplies.

**4.** Vue-All Inc.
P.O. Box 1994, Ocala, FL   32678
Phone (904) 732-3188
Phone Toll Free (800) 874-9737
Fax:  (904) 867-8243
Specializes in good  quality photo sleeves and pages

**5.** Metal Edge West, Inc.
2721 East 45th St., L.A., CA 90058
Phone (213) 588-2228
Phone Toll Free (800) 862-2228
Fax: (213) 588-2150
Internet http://www.eden.com:8080/~midnight/avi/shoppe1.avi
General preservation supplies.

**6.** Light Impressions
439 Monroe Avenue, Rochester, NY   14607-3717
Phone  (716) 271-8960
Phone Toll Free  (800) 828-6216
Fax:  (800) 828-5539
General preservation supplies, scrapbooks and photo albums.

**7.** University Products, Inc.
P.O. Box 101, Holyoke, MA   01041
Phone (413) 532-3372
Phone Toll Free (800) 628-1912
Fax (800) 532- 9281
General preservation supplies, scrapbooks and photo albums.

**8.** Conservation Support Systems
P.O. Box 91746 Santa Barbara, CA   93190
Phone (805) 682-9843
Phone Toll Free (800) 482-6299
Fax:  (805) 682-2064
General preservation supplies.

**9.** Bradley's Plastic Bag Co.
9130 Firestone Blvd. Downey, CA  90241
Phone (213) 923-5556
Phone (818) 289-0811
Phone Toll Free (800) 621-7864
Fax: (310) 862-4474
Plastic supplies of all kinds.

**10.** Archival Products
P.O. Box 1413, Des Moines, IA   50305
Phone Toll Free (800) 247-5323
Fax: (515) 262-6013
General preservation supplies.

**11.** Talas
213 W. 35th St., New York, NY  10001-1996
Phone  (212) 219-0770
Fax: (212) 219-0735
General preservation supplies.  Specializes in textile supplies.

**12.** Conservation Resources
800-H Forbes Place, Springfield, VA   22151
Phone Toll Free (800) 634-6932
Fax:  (703) 321-0629
General preservation supplies.

# CHAPTER 2

## Ceramics, Glass & Other Objects

### *Before a disaster occurs:*

This group of materials suffers the highest amount of damage during an earthquake and will also be affected by heat from fires. The biggest problem with ceramics and glass is, of course, breakage. I have heard so many heart breaking stories about people's cherished broken items and they all have the same despair in their voice; "...what can you do to prevent it? Nothing. Right?" Wrong. Quake Wax.

This material was developed together with scientists at the Getty Museum and they use it. Quake Wax is a sticky synthetic wax that can be used between the base of an small to medium sized object and a table top or shelf to anchor it down. The object can be picked up at any time and Quake Wax will not stain the furniture surface. Other materials, like Plastellina or other "fixing" materials, which contain oil should be avoided as they can stain furniture and objects alike. Use it on decorative plates, curios, porcelain statues in hutches, to make sure they don't rattle around and break against each other during the shake.

I know of a woman, who prior to the Northridge (Los Angeles) earthquake of January 1994, used Quake Wax in her Wilshire Boulevard office and, unbeknownst to her boss, in his office too. During the quake, every person's office on the floor of her office building suffered extreme breakage... every office except her's and her boss's (the building was even condemned!).

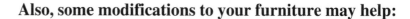

**Also, some modifications to your furniture may help:**

♦ Install clasps or hooks on cabinet doors. They usually pop open, even during a moderate shaker, and let everything inside fall to the floor.

♦ A lip on the front of a shelf will help keep objects in their place. They will have a harder time "walking" off as everything vibrates.

♦ Replace glass shelves in curio cabinets (which will break and crash down on other items... they are heavy too) with Lucite or Plexiglas shelves. They can be made to order at your local glass shop. Help to hold them in place with Quake Wax.

A situation when objects often get broken is during a move from one location to another. I cannot emphasize enough the value to adding some bubble wrap (1/2" - 1" sized bubbles) to the usual newspaper packing method.

**I humbly make the following suggestions for packing anything you don't want broken (this is for items you are moving yourself with care):**

♦ The heavier the items, the sturdier and smaller (lots of heavy items in a big box isn't good for your back either) the box needs to be.

♦ Put a couple of layers of bubble plastic at the bottom of the box.

♦ Wrap bubble plastic around the outside of the newspaper wrapping and tape together.

♦ Pack things tight.

♦ Separate difficult items with pieces of broken (or ripped) cardboard.

Materials may be bought from moving companies or party and paper supply companies. Or ask for a referral from a builder's supply company. Bulk purchases are a lot

Courtesy Gaylord Bros.

Sectioned boxes give good protection for storage...but not enough for shipping.

cheaper than the sizes available from your local home improvement center.

Photographs of individual valuable items and/or a video will be of great help when you have to file an insurance claim. It will also help to put back together badly broken items. Keep a copy at another location.

## *After a disaster occurs:*

After an earthquake, the most important things to remember when picking up the pieces is to carefully protect each fractured piece so that that little chips or edges of the broken shards will not be broken again, chipped or abraded. Pieces should be wrapped in tissue or paper towels and if possible, all chips from a single object should be put together in a single bag or storage box. If a small box is not available for each damaged item, then the padded wrapped pieces can be put into plastic bags and put into a larger box with padding between the bags. Remember to label everything!

It is important to realize that the edges of many broken ceramics will absorb dirt and be stained by liquids. It is imperative to keep the edges clean and protected to insure the best possible repair of the damage. If the ceramics or glass objects are dirty, they can usually be cleaned with water and soap. Generally, it is not best to put broken glass and ceramic items in a dishwasher and great care should be taken during hand washing. Remember to rinse the items very well.

**Be Careful!**

♦ If you are not careful about the cleaning process, ceramics that have cracked glaze will entrap dirt within the cracks and the cracks will become permanently visible.

♦ Some hand painted items, especially miniature portraits, will wash off with water! Yikes! Test first with a cotton swab.

A friend recalls window shopping for figurines at Disneyland with her friend the week before the Northridge Earthquake. Her friend expressed her deep concern for the safety of several Limoge items she had inherited from her mother. She had decided to put them away in a cardboard box and put them out of reach, on the top shelf of a closet. A week later, that cardboard box came crashing down and everything broke to smithereens. What a heartbreak! How to avoid this? Proper and ample packing around each item and/or Quake Wax between the box and the shelf or don't store a box of breakable items up high where it will drop 8 feet.

Courtesy Conservation Materials, Ltd.

I like a soap that comes in a paste called Orvus.

♦ If the broken item is intricate, detailed, or has hand painted artwork on the surface, then it would be better to clean off the dirt and grime with a cotton swab inch by inch.

Simple reassemblage can often be done with white glue. A conservation grade white glue is best. However, household white glues may be used even though they contain impurities which will cause them to yellow in the future. Because white glue will soften when exposed to water, it would be possible to reverse the repairs and do them better in the future. Also for this same reason, any item you glue together with white glue should not be used to cook in nor should it be washed with other dishes in the sink or in the dishwasher. Your item will fall apart again. Therefore, it is recommended that items you glue back together should become decorator objects. You are discouraged from using permanent adhesives like super-glue or epoxies, as these adhesives will yellow and cannot be undone in the future if a better repair needs to be performed. Improperly repaired glass and ceramics with these permanent adhesives are often thrown away in the future.

Putting together small items should not be too much of a problem. Assemblage techniques for numerous broken pieces include using a little tape to see if things fit together first before committing yourself with the glue. For more complicated reassemblage, you may find that large rubber bands will help you to hold pieces together while they are drying.

Courtesy Conservation Materials Ltd.

Another technique is to have a small box of aquarium gravel or clean sand into which you can partially insert your broken item to hold the object in different positions for easier handling during assemblage. Try to resist the temptation of gluing too many pieces together at once.

You may find that the glued sections will begin to sag and then, begin to dry in a distorted shape.

For ceramics, you could try and fill cracks with an artist's gesso and then touch-up along the cracks with acrylic paint. Be sure that you are not painting down inside the cracks with paint. Watercolors may also be safely used.

One of the problems with glass is the way light travels through the object. The pathway of the light is interrupted at a crack or repair area. Unfortunately, there are no products on the supermarket or hardware shelves that can easily be used by the untrained person. From the Conservation Materials Ltd. there is a tube of solvent based synthetic adhesive called B72 which makes the least visible mend, won't yellow and is reversible in solvent. The same adhesive may be used for ceramics.

Contact an object conservation laboratory which specializes in glass items for further consultation for your specific needs.

Ceramics and glass hold up pretty good in a flood situation, if they are not broken. Be careful of hand painted porcelains. It's best to wash off the mud and grime of unglazed pottery as soon as possible. Use a soft brush to help remove globs of mud. Be careful not to rub mud against the surface, as it can be very abrasive and scratch. Otherwise, these items can be cleaned later and there are few problems with drying them off.

If you have antique items or archeological items that were previously repaired, be forewarned that many of those repairs will fall apart in water. If you are dealing with several pieces, wrap in tissue (pad well), store all pieces together in a box or a bag, and be sure to label everything.

The following are a few suggestions for protecting and saving other important family heirlooms:

# Silver Items

There is a difference between old silver (100 years old) and new silver. There are a variety of silver working and polishing techniques that can be damaged by improper cleaning and polishing. You can assume that your silver items have monetary value besides sentimental/heirloom value. These items are worth taking care of.

## *Before a Disaster Occurs:*

**For those items in storage, here are a few guidelines:**

♦ Don't let silver come in contact with stainless steel (it causes a blueing or darkening of the finish).

♦ There are special papers which contain carbon (charcoal) which absorb atmospheric pollutants which cause tarnish.

♦ Metal should never touch metal.

♦ Metal should not be stored in wet conditions.

♦ Wrap the item in tissue paper and put it in a cloth bag (so humidity does not build up inside).

**To protect silver items on shelves:**

♦ All the shelf materials on the market (including some metal shelves), except those of solid wood, give off a chemical gas called formaldehyde. This gas will cause the silver to tarnish and corrode (and it's not good for you either).

Formaldehyde gas can be sealed into the shelf by a good layer of paint on all sides, including the edges. Make sure the paint does not have formaldehyde in it! Even wrapping the shelf with a shelf paper on all sides does much to limit the off-gassing of this toxic material.

♦ Quake Wax will keep items secured in their spots the next time a tremor... or even when a major shake comes to town. The wax material is the

*Never use a silver polish with a tarnish inhibitor. While the tarnish inhibitor may slow down the tarnish return right after you polish the metal, the tarnish will return soon enough... and then it will be much more difficult to get the tarnish off next time. None of the tarnish inhibiters work in any of the products.*

*See explanation of Quake Wax on first page of this chapter.*

same material conservators use to coat metal objects to preserve them and it can be easily removed.

Tremors are not only caused by earthquakes... how about your teenagers... or grandkids!? Anchor things down with Quake Wax and sleep better.

# *After a Disaster Occurs:*

To really look its best, dented, damaged new silver items need to go to a metal worker, who specializes in silver. Old silver requires the expertise of a conservator, if you want to preserve its monetary value and historical appearance.

**In the aftermath:**

1. Pick up the pieces.

2. Wash off the mud and dirt (see instructions that follow).

3. Don't wrap and store wet metal pieces. Be careful. Pieces may have holes with water trapped inside!

4. Wrap pieces in tissue (toilet paper is OK). Metal should never touch metal.

5. Put into a baggie and seal.

6. Label.

7. Take to a conservator (old items) or silversmith (new items).

## *Cleaning and Polishing:*

As I said at the beginning, there's a big difference between old silver and new silver. Knowing the silver working and polishing techniques used on your old item could be the difference between ruining an item and preserving it. Consult with a professional conservator before you decide what to do.

**The following instructions will help you get the mud and dirt off after a disaster:**

1. Try to wash off the dirt under running cool water. Be careful not to scratch the delicate polished surface by wiping away grit and mud.

2. Fill the sink or basin with cool water and add any non-ionic soap. I've heard conservators suggest using Joy or Ivory liquid soap, but the non-ionic soaps will rinse cleaner and won't leave behind deposits.

3. Carefully and slowly swish or dredge the silver item through the soapy water, making sure all areas get washed.

4. Be careful of hollow parts screwed together that can collect water. If you get water inside, set it aside for a couple of days to dry out.

5. Pat or blot dry the surface of the silver with a very soft cloth.

Distilled water would be best, but I'm guessing that after a disaster, you won't be so choosey. Tap water will work.

I like a soap that comes in a paste called Orvus.

Don't put silver through the dishwasher (it will cause uneven streaking and darkening of the finish).

Don't use ammonia in the water. It will react with the silver and tarnish it quickly.

Courtesy Gaylord Bros.

Never use tarnish inhibitors.

You can find this at your local auto supply store.

A wonderful silver cleaning kit is available through the Collector Care series sold by Conservation Materials Ltd. (see suppliers). It was put together after consulting with a number of top silver conservators in the country.

Polishing one's silver is not an easy matter. Everyone would like a quick, easy method. The trouble is that there is not a quick and easy method that doesn't hurt or eat away the silver.

I'm sorry to be the one to tell you that jeweler's rouge is the best polishing method.

**There are some good materials to coat and protect the silver after polishing:**

♦ Carnauba wax paste is used in car waxes, furniture waxes etc. Look at the can and see if it is 100% carnauba wax. That's it. This puts a very hard protective layer on the surface. Two or three layers are much better than one. The down side of this wax is that if you get it gooped up in the crevases or detailed ornamentation, it turns white and you will need to dig it out with a toothpick (just like your car).

♦ Carnauba wax can also be found in liquid form, which won't turn white in the cracks.

♦ Furniture waxes will also work well.

♦ Renaissance Wax has been a wax of choice for those in the know for a long time (See "Where to Buy").

### *Very Important!!:*

Never use a polish with a tarnish inhibitor. A tarnish inhibitor does not work in any of the products and will gravely limit the cleaning and polishing of the item in the future.

Remember, the more you rub it, the more the silver plate comes off. Once cleaned and polished, silver objects should be wrapped in tissue or bagged in cloth bags.

Look through some of the catalogs of the suppliers in the back. They have specialty boxes for storing your objects and protecting them while they are in storage.

# Leather and Rawhide

Leather can be very fragile when wet, especially if it is deteriorated. Be very careful. Rinse with running water or sponge (blot don't rub) with clean water to remove mud and debris. Drying with fans (no heat!) should take place within 48 hours. If your leather is a shaped item, try to pad it to dry it with the same shape (otherwise it will dry out of shape), remembering to change wet pads.

After dry, use a leather reviver on tanned (not chamois, suede or delicate leathers) leathers and buckskins to keep them from cracking and drying out to an extreme.

I was helping to evaluate an estate that was being sold after the death of the owner. In the "pile of stuff" were some very valuable old English silver baskets and trays. The appraiser lamented at seeing the silver worn off so badly by years of zealous polishing. He gave the items perhaps 50% of their value because of the condition.
The heir to the estate, figuring that if the items were replated, they would then not look worn and would recuperate their value. So, after having the items replated, he proudly took them back to the appraiser who shrieked in dismay at the brand new looking pieces. Their character and original silver layers had been ruined. The appraiser took off another 50% of the value.

From Mississippi came the frantic phone call from a lady who was trying to wipe down moldy items with isopropyl alcohol. She had decided to do it on her desk in the living room while watching TV. Unfortunately she knocked over the bottle of alcohol, spilling it onto the desk and onto leather books and photo albums. The solvent ruined the finish on the furniture and permanently stained the leather on the books. What a disaster!

# Basketry, Bone, Hair, Ivory, Shell

If dealing with water damage, expect everything to be very fragile. Any painted designs are very fragile and colors are likely to run. The older it is the easier it falls apart. If colors are stable, then clean off mud and dirt with running water or a sponge can be used to blot away mud or other deposits. Items can be frozen to buy time. Use wax paper between several objects being frozen together.

Once again, these objects need to be dried within 48 hours. Try drying baskets upside down on a pile of dry rags to help them keep their shape while drying. Be sure to change the wet rags.

Photographs of individual valuable items and/or a video will be of great help when you have to file an insurance claim. It will also help to put back together badly broken items. Keep a copy at another location.

Cleaning any old cloth, beaded, sewn, embroidered item should be done with a piece of screen and and a brush ended nozzle.

### *Mold*

Mold doesn't readily grow on hard objects like ceramics, glass, silver, bone, ivory and shell. If you should find mold on those kinds of items, carefully wipe it off with isopropyl alcohol. Be careful if you see hand painting. Test a small place first with a cotton swab to see if the paint rubs off. If it comes off, avoid the painted areas. If it is the painted areas that have mold (which is likely) take your item to a conservator for some help.

Isopropyl alcohol, or any alcohol, will most likely damage the stains on leather. It may also damage the vegetable or plant dyes (colors) on baskets, masks, and other tribal art.

If you have a couple of small mold spots, you may VERY CAREFULLY try to roll on, not rub, a cotton swab with some isopropyl alcohol. Don't insist if it doesn't come off! Your best bet is to seek out a conservator for advice.

There are many judgment calls to be made. Are we talking about a few surface spots of mold on a saddle that can be wiped off with a rag? Or are we talking about an infestation on a pioneer wreath of human hair? If you have any doubts about what you're doing, ask for some advice.

## Supply Locator: Ceramics, Glass & Other Objects

| **Supply** | **Number or Other Resource** |
|---|---|
| | (Numbers correspond to vendor number on next page.) |

| Supply | Number or Other Resource |
|---|---|
| Aquarium gravel or sand (from local pet shop) | Pet shop |
| B72, synthetic solvent | 1, 8 |
| Baggies | 8, Supermarket |
| Boxes, storage | 1, 3, 5, 8 |
| Brushes, paint | 1, 3, 8, Art store |
| Bubble wrap | Moving Co., Paper supply store |
| Cotton swabs | 1, 3, 8, Supermarket, Drug store |
| Cardboard | 5, 8 Moving company, Paper supply store |
| Clasps | 1, Hardware store |
| Fans | Home Improvement, Warehouse store |
| Gesso | 1, 2, 3, 8, Art store |
| Hooks | 1, 2, 3, Hardware store |
| Leather reviver | 1, 3, 7, 8 |
| Lucite | 8, Frame shop, glass company Check with local museum |
| Paper towels | Supermarket |
| Plexiglas | 2, 6, 8, Glass company, Frame shop, Check with local museum |
| Quake wax | 1, 7, 8 |
| Tissue paper | 1, 6, 7, 8, 12, Art store, Drug store |
| Watercolors | 1, Art store |
| White glue | 1, 2, 3, 6, 7, 8, 12 |

NOTE:

"Collector's Care Kits" are available from Conservation Materials, Ltd. for the following:
· Ceramics and Glass
· Silver
· Furniture and Leather

# SUPPLIERS OF PRESERVATION MATERIALS

**When you cannot find what you need at the local store, here is a list of suppliers who will have the hard to find stuff. Call the #800 and ask for a free catalog. They are usually very informative. Also, the lists of materials mentioned from each chapter have numbers that match with the suppliers on this page, so you know who sells what.**

**1.** Conservation Materials Ltd.
Box 2884, Sparks, NV  89431
Phone Toll Free (800) 733-5283
Phone (702) 331-0582
Fax (702) 331-0588
General preservation supplies.  Has Collector Care Kits, scrapbooks and photo albums.

**2.** United Mfrs. Supplies, Inc.
80 Gordon Drive, Syosset, NY 11791
Phone Toll Free  (800) 645-7260
Fax:  (516) 496-7968
Hardware

**3.** Gaylord Archival Preservation & Conservation Supplies and Equipment
Box 4901, Syracuse, NY 13221
Phone Toll Free (800) 448-6160
Fax:  (800) 272-3412
General preservation supplies.

**4.** Vue-All Inc.
P.O. Box 1994, Ocala, FL  32678
Phone (904) 732-3188
Phone Toll Free (800) 874-9737
Fax:  (904) 867-8243
Specializes in good  quality photo sleeves and pages

**5.** Metal Edge West, Inc.
2721 East 45th St., L.A., CA 90058
Phone (213) 588-2228
Phone Toll Free (800) 862-2228
Fax: (213) 588-2150
Internet http://www.eden.com:8080/~midnight/avi/ shoppe1.avi
General preservation supplies.

**6.** Light Impressions
439 Monroe Avenue, Rochester, NY   14607-3717
Phone  (716) 271-8960
Phone Toll Free  (800) 828-6216
Fax:  (800) 828-5539
General preservation supplies, scrapbooks and photo albums.

**7.** University Products, Inc.
P.O. Box 101, Holyoke, MA  01041
Phone (413) 532-3372
Phone Toll Free (800) 628-1912
Fax (800) 532- 9281
General preservation supplies, scrapbooks and photo albums.

**8.** Conservation Support Systems
P.O. Box 91746 Santa Barbara, CA   93190
Phone (805) 682-9843
Phone Toll Free (800) 482-6299
Fax:  (805) 682-2064
General preservation supplies.

**9.** Bradley's Plastic Bag Co.
9130 Firestone Blvd. Downey, CA  90241
Phone (213) 923-5556
Phone (818) 289-0811
Phone Toll Free (800) 621-7864
Fax: (310) 862-4474
Plastic supplies of all kinds.

**10.** Archival Products
P.O. Box 1413, Des Moines, IA   50305
Phone Toll Free (800) 247-5323
Fax: (515) 262-6013
General preservation supplies.

**11.** Talas
213 W. 35th St., New York, NY  10001-1996
Phone  (212) 219-0770
Fax: (212) 219-0735
General preservation supplies.  Specializes in textile supplies.

**12.** Conservation Resources
800-H Forbes Place, Springfield, VA  22151
Phone Toll Free (800) 634-6932
Fax: (703) 321-0629
General preservation supplies.

# CHAPTER 3

## Computer Floppy Disks, Optical Disks, Compact Disks, Sound & Video Recordings

### *Before a disaster occurs:*

It should be remembered that none of these methods of information storage are considered archival or permanent storage media.

**If you have information that is dear to you on these types of materials the very best thing you can do is:**

♦ Make a back-up copy.

♦ Put your originals and copies into proper storage holders (See "Suppliers"). Consult the supplier catalogs.

♦ Keep the copy somewhere else.

♦ Keep originals in clean, dry, cool storage.

Each company that produces these materials has a customer service department that will be happy to tell you the best way to store your cassettes, videos, CDs and diskettes. Look on the packaging to see if there is an #800 number or call 1-800-555-1212 to ask the toll free information operator the number of the company you want. If they have something written to send you, great. Otherwise write down their suggestions and do your best to follow through. However, even if you have great storage, you should still make duplicates. By the way, the manufacturer's phone numbers will also come in handy when a disaster occurs and you need some technical help.

*Courtesy Gaylord Bros.*

Acid free buffered boxes will protect your record jackets. Note the cotton gloves.

**Manufacturer's precautions include:**

- Don't touch the electronic media surface with fingers (oils and grime are bad).

- Avoid direct sunlight and hot days in locked, closed up cars.

- Avoid extreme heat.

- Avoid banging them around town. Keep shock/impact to a minimum.

- Avoid magnetic sources (it can wipe out some data).

- Don't put them through the X ray machine at the airport (or the doctor's office).

- Do not get them wet.

## *After a disaster occurs:*

**Do not, under any circumstances, use:**

- Bleaches

- Detergents

- Fungicides

- Disinfectants

Earthquakes result in shock/impact and likely a lot of dirt and dust. The casing may be damaged but the storage media may be OK. Consult with local experts in computer or video duplication stores and have a copy (or two) made. Having a copy made is better than trying to blow out dirt, wash or repair, which may all result in further or complete loss of recorded information.

### *Water damage and floods:*

You're in trouble. As with everything else, mold is a big enemy. But in addition, you also have to consider the plastic casing the tapes/disks are housed in. If the housing is no longer functional, the tape is often no longer useable and you will require the assistance of technicians to copy the information to another storage media. Basically, what you want to do is get the item cleaned up or

Courtesy Gaylord Bros.

New acid free buffered boxes provide clean storage for sensitive audio tapes.

dried out sufficiently to get a copy made and then throw the original away. Here are a few more precise details:

## Floppy Disks:

The disk is made of iron oxide bonded to a polyester film, housed in plastic sleeves lined with Tyvek (tm). If wet for too long, the iron oxide, which carries the encoded information, will be disturbed.

## Immediate response on your part is needed:

♦ Either the diskette needs to be dried out quickly and evenly or...

♦ The diskette needs to be kept wet until it can be dried properly.

♦ What to do:

♦ Damp diskettes can be dried with a blow dryer on a low heat setting.

♦ If there are too many to work on quickly, they should be kept wet in clean cold water in clean containers. Make sure you change the water daily.

♦ Several of the major disk manufacturers will provide salvage information and techniques. Call them!

Your potential recovery rate will be very low depending on how wet, for how long and how dirty the water was.

## Videotapes:

If your family films have gotten damp, then try to blow them dry with a blow dryer on low or no heat. Otherwise, look in the yellow pages under "Video duplicating and transfer service" or other kind of video production lab and maybe they will be able to reproduce the tape for you. Another option might be to ask a film lab that works with movie film to see if they can chemically dry and clean the tape in a way that would make reproduction possible.

Courtesy Gaylord Bros.

Polyethylene record sleeves offer great protection against scratches.

**Compact disks, video disks, records, etc.:**

♦ Normally these can be washed in clean water and air dried without too many problems.

♦ Direct sunlight or a hot air from an hair dryer will cause the plastic of the disk to warp.

♦ Be extra careful if there is mud as these disks will scratch like a record.

♦ Reproduction is recommended especially if you have important data or family photos stored.

## *Supply Locator: Computer Floppy Disks, Optical Disks, Compact Disks, Sound & Video Recordings*

**Supply**                                           **Number or Other Resource**

(Numbers correspond to vendor number on next page.)

Boxes, acid free archival .................................................. 1, 3, 5, 6, 7, 8, 10, 12
Boxes, plastic (Tupperware or Rubbermaid) ............... Supermarket, Warehouse store

# SUPPLIERS OF PRESERVATION MATERIALS

**When you cannot find what you need at the local store, here is a list of suppliers who will have the hard to find stuff. Call the #800 and ask for a free catalog. They are usually very informative. Also, the lists of materials mentioned from each chapter have numbers that match with the suppliers on this page, so you know who sells what.**

**1.** Conservation Materials Ltd.
Box 2884, Sparks, NV  89431
Phone Toll Free (800) 733-5283
Phone (702) 331-0582
Fax (702) 331-0588
General preservation supplies.  Has Collector Care Kits, scrapbooks and photo albums.

**2.** United Mfrs. Supplies, Inc.
80 Gordon Drive, Syosset, NY 11791
Phone Toll Free  (800) 645-7260
Fax:  (516) 496-7968
Hardware

**3.** Gaylord Archival Preservation & Conservation
Supplies and Equipment
Box 4901, Syracuse, NY 13221
Phone Toll Free (800) 448-6160
Fax:  (800) 272-3412
General preservation supplies.

**4.** Vue-All Inc.
P.O. Box 1994, Ocala, FL   32678
Phone (904) 732-3188
Phone Toll Free (800) 874-9737
Fax:  (904) 867-8243
Specializes in good  quality photo sleeves and pages

**5.** Metal Edge West, Inc.
2721 East 45th St., L.A., CA 90058
Phone (213) 588-2228
Phone Toll Free (800) 862-2228
Fax: (213) 588-2150
Internet http://www.eden.com:8080/~midnight/avi/
shoppe1.avi
General preservation supplies.

**6.** Light Impressions
439 Monroe Avenue, Rochester, NY   14607-3717
Phone  (716) 271-8960
Phone Toll Free  (800) 828-6216
Fax:  (800) 828-5539
General preservation supplies, scrapbooks and photo albums.

**7.** University Products, Inc.
P.O. Box 101, Holyoke, MA   01041
Phone (413) 532-3372
Phone Toll Free (800) 628-1912
Fax (800) 532- 9281
General preservation supplies, scrapbooks and photo albums.

**8.** Conservation Support Systems
P.O. Box 91746 Santa Barbara, CA   93190
Phone (805) 682-9843
Phone Toll Free (800) 482-6299
Fax:  (805) 682-2064
General preservation supplies.

**9.** Bradley's Plastic Bag Co.
9130 Firestone Blvd. Downey, CA  90241
Phone (213) 923-5556
Phone (818) 289-0811
Phone Toll Free (800) 621-7864
Fax: (310) 862-4474
Plastic supplies of all kinds.

**10.** Archival Products
P.O. Box 1413, Des Moines, IA   50305
Phone Toll Free (800) 247-5323
Fax: (515) 262-6013
General preservation supplies.

**11.** Talas
213 W. 35th St., New York, NY  10001-1996
Phone  (212) 219-0770
Fax: (212) 219-0735
General preservation supplies.  Specializes in textile supplies.

**12.** Conservation Resources
800-H Forbes Place, Springfield, VA   22151
Phone Toll Free (800) 634-6932
Fax: (703) 321-0629
General preservation supplies.

# CHAPTER 4

# Paper Items

### *Before a disaster occurs:*

If your water heater leaked all over the garage floor and your storage boxes of "stuff" got wet, what would be damaged? Worthless stuff? Probably not. Important letters, certificates, the kid's school work are all things that make up your family's history and deserve to be protected.

**The first step in their preservation is to get the important things out of your cardboard boxes and put them in a safer place, even temporarily.**

- Get them out of the cardboard box.

- Put them into a clean acid-free buffered archival box from one of the suppliers in the back list or even a waterproof container like Rubbermaid or Tupperware from your large drugstore or discount warehouse.

- Make sure the box is labeled both lid and bottom.

- Find a safe, dry, cool place to store the boxes.

"Where do I start!"

The next step in side stepping a disaster is to make a copy of all your important things. Take an inventory of what is important to you. I mean really important, like birth certificates, passports, diplomas, legal documents (bank records, wills etc.).

But be careful! If you don't protect the items during your trip to the photocopier, you may have a disaster! Put them in an envelope, holder, whatever... just protect them against blowing away or getting the corners bent or folded while handling them. Try page protectors (read about them a couple of paragraphs ahead). They work great.

*See the Chapter "Making Copies"*

Make a couple of good photocopies of everything and keep one copy at a relative's house and keep another copy in a plastic container somewhere at home. When traveling, make copies of passports, traveler's checks, plane tickets and such and put a set in each suitcase. When "disaster" hits, have a backup.

## *Fading:*

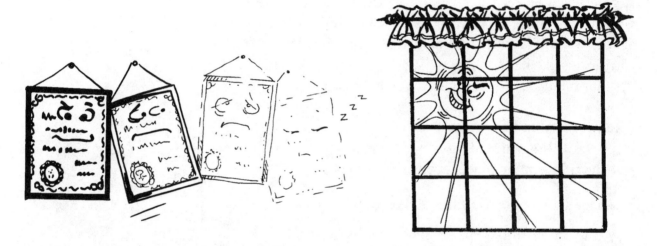

*Going, going, gone... especially hand written letters and signatures.*

In short, don't put anything up on the wall and in the light that is important to you. (How about framing a copy? See the section on "Making Copies.") The light doesn't have to be direct sunlight in order to cause fading. Fluorescent lights fade in rooms where no sunlight exists at all.

**Some items will fade faster than others. Some of the most sensitive are:**

♦ Signatures and writing in ballpoint pen are the most sensitive.

- Writing inks in general.

- Watercolors.

- Many color prints, like lithographs, will change color, especially under fluorescent lights.

Glass does not filter out ultraviolet light (which causes fading). There are types of glass or acrylic "glass" that reduce the amount of fading but do not eliminate it (UF3 Plexiglas, Museum Glass, True Vue; see your framer or plexi supplier). Window tinting can be purchased with a UV filter: this helps.

Color photography that changes color is not fading because of light. The chemistry of the print is unstable and it will continue to change even in the dark. To preserve a photo that is changing color, take a new picture of your old picture (before the color goes too far out of whack) and make a new print. If this sounds like Greek to you, call a color photo lab and ask for help (look under "Photo Finishing" in the yellow pages).

**In order to protect the original papers, follow these steps:**

- Place important papers in archival plastic page protectors.

- Use acid-free buffered paper storage materials or the correct kind of plastic materials.

- Place page protectors in a notebook.

The correct plastic used for the pages should be polyester, polypropylene or polyethylene. Bad materials to be avoided are polyvinylchloride (PVC) or anything that smells weird or strong. Only the approved plastics will not transfer, or pull the letters off your photocopy onto the plastic.

The 8 1/2" X 11" pages that I am recommending are clear plastic and your letter is slid in from the top or side. Page protectors come divided into sections so you can store

After her husband was killed in a car accident, a dear friend was going through "paper work" and was hit with the realization that many papers and certificates were more than just papers in a file. They were important for her two kids to have. They told about their father.

This realization changed the way my friend began to recognize what kinds of items make up her "family history."

Mr. Acid Free Buffered: Here to protect your family history!

several, say baseball cards, to a page. You can even economize by putting things in the sleeves back to back. If you do this though, you won't be able to read anything that's written on the back.

I don't recommend taking the time now to organize all your papers into years or other categories. Perhaps a very general categorizing of papers wouldn't be too time-consuming but don't get bogged down in a big project now or you won't finish this emergency preparedness effort in a timely manner. Just do a general categorizing and get them into the page protectors. You could write on the top of each page a note about the identification, date or from where you got the item.

Call the suppliers in the Appendix for free catalogs. Without a doubt, you will find something to meet your needs and at good prices.

Also, don't worry at this point about the rips, stains, folds, etc. While going about these prevention tasks, it is not the time to work on them. The page protectors will do their job. They will prevent even the ugliest rip from getting worse. Just get through this job as quickly and as thoroughly as possible.

Order the page protectors, 100 to a package (bulk/wholesale) through a mail order company (see "Suppliers"). I have also bought them every once in awhile at the large warehouses like Price/Costco. Inquire around. You may be able to get them at stores like Fedco or Walmart. Prices range from about $ .18 to $ .50 per page for the exact same type of page.

Courtesy Gaylord Bros.

Safe and sound: In protective sleeves and stored in an acid free buffered box...and still easy to get to.

**For your other odd sized papers that don't fit into a page protector, you will need:**

♦ To buy a special archival plastic folder, file folder, map folder or Mylar envelope like "L"velope or...

♦ You can put them into acid-free buffered manila envelopes.

♦ Also, many items can be put into a single box or archival shoe box with acid-free buffered separating sheets.

♦ Refer to the supply houses and their catalogs listed at the end of the book.

Once you have filled your archival quality page protectors, any school plastic covered notebook will do for keeping the page protectors, even though the notebook is not archival quality. The papers are safe in their pages and the notebook won't hurt them. Don't use a notebook with a cloth cover; as the colors can run if the notebook gets wet and the dye will run all over staining everything. Be sure to label what is in the notebook.

Congratulations!!! You have just turned the tables in your favor on the destiny and preservation of your treasured family history items.

**By taking these steps to separate and safeguard your most important papers, you have made sure that they will not:**

◆ Cause each other to yellow because of acids.

◆ Stick together if it gets humid.

◆ Run colors or inks together if they get wet (although if water gets into the page protector, you've got troubles).

◆ Get smudged, wrinkled, bent or torn when being handled.

The improvement in your storage will especially be good for your most fragile and beat up papers. If your treasured document is torn badly and very brittle, it may be best to lie it prone in an archival box.

If you are going to put the notebooks full of certificates and letters into storage, (you won't be getting them out very often to look through them) I suggest you get a large plastic (polyethylene) container (like Rubbermaid or Tupperware) with a lid that does not seal. They can be closed to keep out bugs and varmints. You can even tape it shut, but if you seal the container, condensation may occur, then you will get mold. Also, these heavy-duty containers will fare better in an earthquake. Do not store

Acidic paper goes yellow, becomes stained, embrittles and breaks apart. Notice the breaks along the fold lines from being kept in its envelope.

If you have something like this, put it into a page protector, lie it flat in a box and take it to a conservator. Don't let it slide around... pieces will break off.

them in the attic where heat will embrittle, cause discoloration and cause colors to change. Keep them in a cool, dry place.

Another big plus, is that in the event of a disaster which involves water, you will have the papers stored in a clean manner. Cardboard boxes and the like not only soak up water, but the cardboard itself will bleed off impurities when wet and the yellowing will be carried by the water to stain everything else around. Your foresight will keep this from happening.

Once again, I recommend photocopying everything that's important and keeping a copy at someone else's home. (see "Making Copies")

## *After a disaster occurs:*

**Let's say you have a water problem and your stuff is in the water. The first thing to do is:**

1. Get the water to stop (as if you needed to to be told that!).

2. Go over building and personal safety checklists (see lists in Appendix).

3. Begin salvage efforts by getting small piles of papers out of the water.

4. But don't try to lift large wet paper items out of drawers or from the water. They will rip to shreds.

5. Sponge out the water first.

6. Let the large items dry (circulating air) in the drawer.

Wet paper falls apart easily. If you must handle a sheet of wet paper, a good suggestion is to get a sheet of good strong paper towel and lay the wet piece of paper on the paper toweling and move both of the sheets together. The best choice for a paper towel would be the thickest towel possible that holds together when wet and has the least amount of texture to it. Pick the towel that is as lint-free as possible and if possible, plain white (no bunnies, flowers, or hearts).

Russell Krueger demonstrates the results of his 5th grade class research: The best paper towel. The winner? Bounty. Holds tough when wet!

## *How to dry wet papers*

### Do not under any circumstances use:

- ♦ Bleaches

- ♦ Detergents

- ♦ Fungicides

- ♦ Disinfectants

- ♦ Staples or paper clips on wet paper

### Follow these tips when drying paper pieces:

1. A piece of wet or damp paper can be dried between sheets of paper toweling by putting one or two sheets of absorbent paper towels (no colors, no texture, no perfumes) on each side of the wet piece of paper to be dried (be sure there are no folds in the paper document or in the paper towels or the folds will be made permanent once the whole is put under pressure to dry).

2. Place a clean board (possibly a kitchen cutting board) or a book on top as a weight. If you use a book, it should be larger than the item being dried.

Dried water stains...you can't do anything about them. Consult a professional conservator.

3. IMPORTANT: Place a sheet of wax paper, or plastic between the books and the paper towels being dried so the books don't absorb the water.

4. Once the paper towels have absorbed water from the papers being dried, they can be set aside to dry and reused later (dry them in another area so as not to add moisture to the air). Once the paper towels begin to get dirty and collect stains from the papers that are being dried, they can be thrown away.

5. Do not rub, clean, or try to fix papers while they are wet.

6. If you feel particularly skilled with your hands, you may want to try to align rips before putting them between paper toweling and under books to dry. A small blade or flat utensil will be helpful when trying to move the delicate paper fibers into place.

The drying cycle of exchanging dry paper towels for wet ones should be repeated for at least a couple of days until the papers are dry. If you take the papers out from under the book/weights before they are perfectly dry, they will distort or warp.

Once again, it is important to keep cool air circulating and to dry them out as soon as possible in order to keep mold growth at a minimum.

### What About Mold?

Mold is one of the more severe problems you will have to deal with after your papers have gotten wet and stayed damp. This is why it is so important to take action as soon as possible after the unfortunate disaster. Once your papers become infested, it will be hard to get rid of.

**Let me summarize what I have already written with a list of what you can do to minimize mold problems:**

♦ Set up fans to circulate the air; no heat.

♦ Separate sheets of paper, don't leave them in piles. Try setting them on butcher paper to help wick out the water. Be careful! Wet paper falls apart easily.

♦ Dry the items within 72 hours, no direct sun or heaters, and in a closed area or...

♦ Freeze all items that cannot be dried.

**If your papers are afflicted by a little mold or mildew on the surface:**

1. Get them dry as soon as possible (moldy items are high priority!). This stuff grows fast!

2. Protect yourself with a face mask with a carbon filter (mold spores are very small and may penetrate regular dust masks). Some people are allergic to mold.

3. Outside, away from other papers, photos etc., remove the surface mold with a very soft, clean brush or...

4. Brush the mold into the nozzle of your vacuum cleaner and be sure to clean the brush off well after you are done so that you don't transfer mold to another item later.

5. Don't let the mold dust get on anything else or later, when the humidity rises, the mold spores that have settled will grow again.

6. If there is a residue on the surface of the paper, take a cotton swab and wipe the surface with isopropyl alcohol. This should remove the mold and may even kill some of it.

The more severe the problem, the more you will need professional help. The older the photo, the more urgently you will need a specialized professional.

Separate papers when they get wet or they will grow mold more easily.

Read the section on drying

### Can't Treat it? Freeze it!

If a large quantity of papers has become wet and drying them out immediately is not possible, then place them in a large plastic container (Tupperware, plastic milk crates) or in the large freezer bags and put the piles of paper in a freezer (rent space in a commercial freezer if you are really in trouble) within 48 hours. They will wait there patiently until they can be treated.

- ♦ Piles of paper should be separated with a sheet of wax paper, as you put them into boxes or bags.

- ♦ Don't try and separate each individual sheet, as the handling of single wet sheets of paper can be very difficult!

- ♦ Handle with care!

- ♦ Check local commercial services for freeze drying.

### Repairing Rips

Dry, torn paper really isn't an "emergency." It won't grow mold or get worse if you are careful. You can always fix it later when the emergency situation passes. In the meantime, you can protect torn and damaged papers with archival quality plastic page protectors, acid-free buffered paper folders or something similar.

If you're losing sleep over a ripped document, the following procedure may help you relax. The steps to be taken will need to be applied more delicately if the ripped paper is thin. Or you may have to repeat some steps if the paper is thick and stiff.

### To repair ripped paper:

1. Take a DAMP cotton swab (distilled water) and,

2. Roll the swab along the fold, crease or distortion. Be careful not to roll up the paper on the cotton swab...

3. Do not saturate the paper, but instead apply light humidity on both sides of the wrinkled area.

The static cling between the two sheets of a Mylar envelope (like "L"velopes) will hold the torn paper together. It may look good enough that you will forget it's torn.

4. Place the page between sheets of absorbent paper toweling and put a book on top (with wax paper) to let the page dry under pressure. See directions for drying papers.

5. Once the page has been dried and the edges have been realigned, then a reversible archival document repair tape can be used for local temporary repair. See "Where to Buy" and "Suppliers", and follow the directions on box.

6. DO NOT USE TAPE!!!!!!!!!!!!!

7. Put your repaired item into a page protector or appropriate envelope/holder.

8. Get a good nights sleep.

I like the Archival Aid's mending tissue best.

## *Cleaning Dirty Paper*

**Do not under any circumstances use:**

♦ Bleaches

♦ Detergents

♦ Fungicides

♦ Disinfectants

♦ Staples or paper clips on wet paper

♦ Before cleaning, make sure the paper is very dry.

♦ Wash your hands before handling papers and keep them clean during the cleaning process by washing and thoroughly drying.

Dirty paper may not be an emergency situation. It won't get worse, especially if it is in a page protector. So cleaning, like rip repair, would be a second or third priority thing to do.

**Once everything else is saved from the disaster and safe...**

1. Clear a flat, clean work area.

2. Use an architectural eraser sack, or crumbled eraser.

Crumbled eraser pads for cleaning dust and grime off the surface. It does not remove stains or yellowing.

3. Sprinkle a little on the surface and massage the paper's surface.

4. Do not rub vigorously. Do not insist in areas of pencil writing or drawing.

5. You will notice the color of the eraser material changing darker as it picks up dirt.

6. Brush off the eraser and dust with a very soft brush (1" - 4" natural bristle paint brush, very clean or new, will work fine).

7. Or vacuum up the eraser and dust through a clean window screen laid over the paper item with a brush tipped vacuum nozzle.

8. Put into archival quality page protectors or other archival holder.

A solid eraser (vs. the crumbled eraser) is also often used but there is a greater risk of crunching or wrinkling (damaging) the paper.

**If you are going to use a solid eraser:**

♦ Buy a vinyl eraser, not a rubber one.

♦ Don't rub vigorously.

♦ It's easy to abrade the paper (that's bad).

♦ Rub from the center of the paper towards the edge.

♦ Vacuum up the eraser stuff through a clean window screen laid over the paper item with a brush tipped vacuum nozzle or brush off with a soft brush.

♦ Pencil marks come off faster with solid erasers... Be careful.

♦ Put into archival quality page protectors or other archival holder.

Another interesting cleaning material is called a Groomstick. It isn't an eraser but instead, it kind of absorbs up the dirt. It's soft and can be rubbed on or rolled over the surface without the risk of abrading the paper.

Using a solid eraser...
Vinyl erasers better than rubber

Courtesy Conservation Materials, Ltd.

Using a Groomstick...

You can still crunch or wrinkle the paper though, so be careful. One of the nice things about the Groomstick is that it doesn't leave behind a residue nor is there anything to wipe off or vacuum up.

While handling a lot of different pages, it is important to wear gloves so as not to transfer the dirt from page to page. Recommended gloves for this use are polyethylene surgical gloves or white cotton gloves (See "Where to Buy").

These types of treatments, when cautiously performed, will be good for use on letters, certificates, documents, magazine pages, newspaper articles, photographs, etc.

A lady came into the office one day, all in a panic about the cleaning she had been doing on her family documents. Her well-intentioned, overzealous hard work had erased all the signatures that were written in pencil!

# *Supply Locator: Paper Items*

| **Supply** | **Number or Other Resource** |
|---|---|
| | (Numbers correspond to vendor number on next page.) |
| Bags, large freezer | 6, 7, 8, Supermarket |
| Boxes, acid free archival | 1, 3, 5, 6, 7, 8, 10, 12 |
| Brushes, natural bristle paint | 1, 3, 7, 8, 12, Paint store |
| Envelopes, manila, acid free buffered | 1, 3, 5, 6, 7, 8, 12 |
| Erasers, crumbled | 1, 3, 8, 12, Art store |
| Erasers, gum | 1, 3, 8, Art store |
| Eraser sack, architectural | 1, 2, 3, 8, 12, Art store |
| Folders, archival plastic, file, map, "L"velope | 1, 2, 3, 5, 6, 7, 8, 10, 12 |
| Gloves, cotton | 1, 2, 3, 7, 8, 12 |
| Gloves, polyethylene surgical | 3, 7, 8, Medical supply |
| Milk crates, plastic | Home Improvement, Warehouse store |
| Notebooks, school plastic covered | 1, 3, Office Supply store |
| Page protectors, archival plastic | 2, 3, 5, 6, 7, 8, 12 |
| Paper, storage materials, acid free | 3, 5, 6, 7, 8, 10, 12 |
| Plastic boxes (Tupperware or Rubbermaid) | Supermarket, Drug store, Warehouse store |
| Plastic, wrap, sheets | 7, Hardware store, Construction supply |
| Separating sheets, acid free, buffered | 1, 3, 5, 7, 8, 12 |
| Screen, window | Hardware store |
| Shoe box, archival | 1, 3, 5, 6, 7, 8, 12 |
| Swabs, cotton | 1, 3, 8, Supermarket, Drug store |
| Tape, reversible archival document | 1, 3, 6, 7, 8, 12 |
| Towels, paper | Supermarket |
| Water, distilled | Supermarket |
| Wax paper | Supermarket |

# SUPPLIERS OF PRESERVATION MATERIALS

**When you cannot find what you need at the local store, here is a list of suppliers who will have the hard to find stuff. Call the #800 and ask for a free catalog. They are usually very informative. Also, the lists of materials mentioned from each chapter have numbers that match with the suppliers on this page, so you know who sells what.**

**1.** Conservation Materials Ltd.
Box 2884, Sparks, NV 89431
Phone Toll Free (800) 733-5283
Phone (702) 331-0582
Fax (702) 331-0588
General preservation supplies. Has Collector Care Kits, scrapbooks and photo albums.

**2.** United Mfrs. Supplies, Inc.
80 Gordon Drive, Syosset, NY 11791
Phone Toll Free (800) 645-7260
Fax: (516) 496-7968
Hardware

**3.** Gaylord Archival Preservation & Conservation
Supplies and Equipment
Box 4901, Syracuse, NY 13221
Phone Toll Free (800) 448-6160
Fax: (800) 272-3412
General preservation supplies.

**4.** Vue-All Inc.
P.O. Box 1994, Ocala, FL 32678
Phone (904) 732-3188
Phone Toll Free (800) 874-9737
Fax: (904) 867-8243
Specializes in good quality photo sleeves and pages

**5.** Metal Edge West, Inc.
2721 East 45th St., L.A., CA 90058
Phone (213) 588-2228
Phone Toll Free (800) 862-2228
Fax: (213) 588-2150
Internet http://www.eden.com:8080/~midnight/avi/
shoppe1.avi
General preservation supplies.

**6.** Light Impressions
439 Monroe Avenue, Rochester, NY 14607-3717
Phone (716) 271-8960
Phone Toll Free (800) 828-6216
Fax: (800) 828-5539
General preservation supplies, scrapbooks and photo albums.

**7.** University Products, Inc.
P.O. Box 101, Holyoke, MA 01041
Phone (413) 532-3372
Phone Toll Free (800) 628-1912
Fax (800) 532- 9281
General preservation supplies, scrapbooks and photo albums.

**8.** Conservation Support Systems
P.O. Box 91746 Santa Barbara, CA 93190
Phone (805) 682-9843
Phone Toll Free (800) 482-6299
Fax: (805) 682-2064
General preservation supplies.

**9.** Bradley's Plastic Bag Co.
9130 Firestone Blvd. Downey, CA 90241
Phone (213) 923-5556
Phone (818) 289-0811
Phone Toll Free (800) 621-7864
Fax: (310) 862-4474
Plastic supplies of all kinds.

**10.** Archival Products
P.O. Box 1413, Des Moines, IA 50305
Phone Toll Free (800) 247-5323
Fax: (515) 262-6013
General preservation supplies.

**11.** Talas
213 W. 35th St., New York, NY 10001-1996
Phone (212) 219-0770
Fax: (212) 219-0735
General preservation supplies. Specializes in textile supplies.

**12.** Conservation Resources
800-H Forbes Place, Springfield, VA 22151
Phone Toll Free (800) 634-6932
Fax: (703) 321-0629
General preservation supplies.

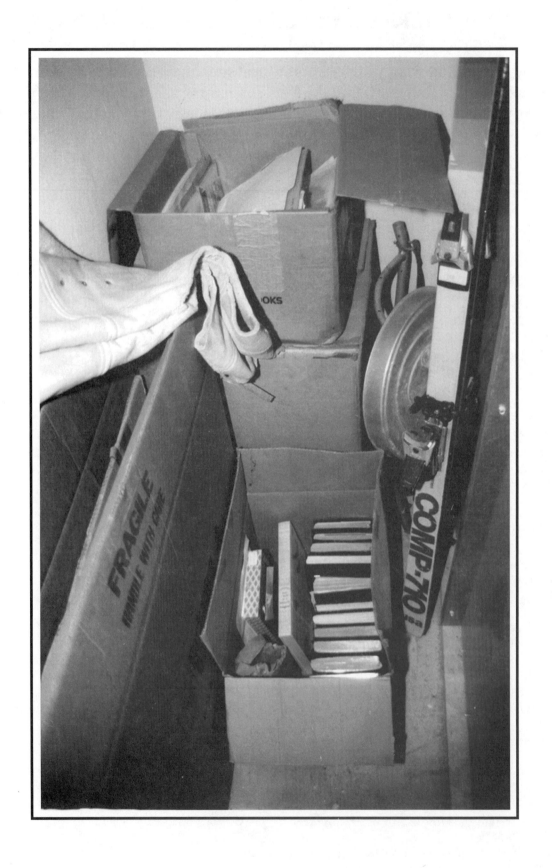

# CHAPTER 5

## Books

*Before a disaster occurs:*

I would guess that everyone has cardboard boxes of books that are being stored. If your boxes got wet, what would you lose... novels and old National Geographics waiting for a new book shelf to be built? Are your journals, yearbooks and family bible stored with the worthless stuff, boxed on the garage floor waiting for the water heater to leak? My point is that a good place to start preventing damage to your most important books is to select them out of your storage boxes and put them in a safer place. I'm sure you have room somewhere in the house for a small flat box (Tupperware) or two...perhaps under the bed or up in the closet? Make sure the box is labeled on the bottom and the lid.

Books can be in poor condition because they are made of poor materials or because they have been treated poorly. Either way, a book in fragile condition is going to be damaged quickly if you have a disaster. Your old book in poor condition is not going to give you time to save it. It will fall immediately apart.

Any really important book deserves its own book box. Slip covers offer some protection but they can cause damage to brittle old books when sliding them in and out. This will help protect the book from handling, dust, light and from other books sliding against it. Look in the cata-

Read the section on "Paper Items" for additional information.

The book most often brought to my college class on the evening we talk about books is the family Bible, full of writing and memories.

logs of suppliers (see "Suppliers") and you will see lots of options for boxes. Measure your book and pick the closest size available (bigger). The sales rep on the other end of the 800 # should be helpful.

**To protect your books against earthquake damage, do the following:**

♦ Install clasps or hooks on cabinet doors. They usually pop open, even during a moderate shaker, and let everything inside fall to the floor.

♦ Use Quake Wax to hold adjustable shelves in place, especially glass ones.

♦ During a good shaker tall or top heavy furniture (full of books) will topple over. Behind the furniture, install anchor bolts (long eye screws) into the studs (not just into the plaster) and tie the furniture to the wall with a nylon coated wire. This type of wire can be bought in the form of picture hanging wire in heavy gauge. Nylon coated wire won't rust and the picture hanging wire is specially treated to be extra strong in relation to it's thickness or gauge. See "where to buy" at end of book.

♦ A lip on the front of the book shelf without doors will help keep books in their place. They will have a harder time "walking" off the shelf as everything vibrates.

## *After a disaster occurs:*

Books (which are dry) caught in fires, earthquakes, hurricanes or whatever that have been recovered, just need to be dusted off with a soft brush (wear particle dust paper mask- but if you want greater protection, wear a paper mask with a carbon filter) and set in a safe place so you can get to them when you have time.

Wet books are extremely fragile. When you are trying to salvage books from water, old books pose a different problem than new books. Broken spines and bindings, brittle and yellowed pages and dissolved glues make handling

*See "where to buy" at end of the chapter.*

*Photographs of individual valuable items and/or a video will be of great help when you have to file an insurance claim. Keep a copy at another location.*

the books a difficult and risky task. If you are not careful your saving efforts could result in more damage through handling than through the disaster which you have recently experienced.

**Action must be taken within 72 hours or mold will become your constant companion.**

- The first thing you need to do is get fresh circulating air (open a window and turn on a couple of fans) into the room as soon as possible. (Call a rental company for a commercial dehumidifier).

- Do not turn on the heat.

**Wet books are a difficult problem for two reasons:**

If your books are wet, you don't have time to just let them sit.

- One, is that a book contains many materials that mold and mildew love to eat, and...

- Two, they are hard to dry out because they are thick.

**Words of caution:**

- Glues, adhesives, book bindings, and paper become very fragile and will fall apart without much encouragement when wet.

There is a difference between "wet" books (that drip and feel definitely wet) and damp books (which can even feel almost dry).

- Paper may fall apart easily or tear easily when substantially humid even if it does not feel wet.

- Because of all the different materials that make up the construction of a spine of a book, swelling can take place. Do not tightly close wet books that are open. You will break the spines, sewing, etc.

- Do not open up wide wet books that are closed for the same reason. The soft materials in the construction will break.

- Old deteriorated leather book covers will fall apart easily or abrade easily.

If you are involved in a general disaster and have a lot of books to save, pick your fight:
Do you need to save all your books? Don't worry about the books that can be replaced with a new one. In the hurry of a disaster, save your best books, your most important books:

* The family bible
* Journals
* Accounting
* Family heirlooms
* Investments

♦ New book covers on glossy paper may stick together. Keep them apart!

♦ Cloth book covers may have colors that run. This will stain the pages of every book close by.

Handling a wet book requires the utmost attention and care.

### Drying wet books

**Do not, under any circumstances, use:**

♦ Bleaches

♦ Detergents

♦ Fungicides

♦ Disinfectants

♦ Staples or paper clips on wet paper

If you have one or two books that are wet, then you can take sheets of white paper towel and put them between the pages of the book (be careful about handling wet paper... it rips very easily, especially if it is old!), about one every few pages.

1. Use wet strength paper toweling.

2. Use one paper towel every few pages.

3. Do not do more than 10 towels at a time.

4. Change the toweling as it gets wet. If the paper towel is not dirty, let it dry out and reuse it later. If the paper towels do not become wet (they may be only slightly damp), then they can be replaced every couple of hours.

5. Do not rub the wet pages as the paper fibers will pull apart easily thereby damaging the page and inks.

6. Leave the book closed while drying with the paper towels.

Damp books can be left on the shelf, opened to about 45 degrees, to dry if there is circulating air.

**It is very important that a book be dried as quickly as possible.**

- Try putting your book on cookie racks to allow air to circulate on all sides.

- A fan will help move the air. Do not use a heater unless ample fresh air is being brought in and never let the books get hot.

- High humidity and added heat will encourage the growth of mold, which will occur very quickly.

A word about soggy periodicals and books on glossy papers: Be careful, they fall apart easily. Keep wet magazines closed tight and freeze dry them for best results. Pack large numbers of them the same way as books: spine down, tightly packed (but be careful not to rub them against each other and abrade the covers, which may have nice illustrations that could be damaged).

**Be extra attentive of books with glossy covers and pages (coated paper):**

- The pages will stick together easily if dried while the book is closed.

- Print will slide off the page if it is rubbed.

- Keep the book submerged in clean water till it can be dried, page by page.

- Rewetting a dried book almost never works (it stays stuck together).

- Freeze drying these kinds of papers is hardly ever successful.

No hot hair dryers on leather bindings. Heat will ruin leather and help dissolve wet glues.

See "Where to Buy" and "Supplier" lists.

Courtesy Gaylord Bros.

**If an important magazine has fallen apart:**

1. Gather together all the pages.

2. Use a sling of wet strength paper towel or a clean window screen to help move the papers.

3. Dry out the pages (see instructions for drying wet papers).

4. Store dried pages where they won't be disturbed (in page protectors).

5. Take the loose pages to a book binder to have him put it back together. It shouldn't cost very much. Call your local library for a referral or consult your Yellow Pages.

**Books bound in leather, vellum and parchment which have gotten wet:**

1. Blot dry with clean rags or paper towels.

2. Do not try to dry leather book-covers with blow dryers as humidity and high temperatures will cause the leather to deteriorate quickly and become very brittle.

**Once the book bindings have been dried by circulating air (with fans) leather treatment materials can be used to revive the quality of the leather.**

1. Collagen based leather reviver can be used first.

2. When the leather reviver has absorbed into the leather and the surface is dry, carnauba waxes, which protect the surface, can be used.

3. Follow up with tinted waxes for touch-ups.

If the leather has been ripped or torn, do not attempt to glue the leather back together. The rip will not go back together evenly. It may dry crooked. You may damage the leather so that it cannot be done properly later. Before you try anything, a professional book conservator is your first choice for phone consultation. The good advice you will get won't cost you anything. A book binder is a distant second choice. Old fashioned book covers made of grocery bags will do much to protect a worn, fragile book cover until proper protection and restoration can be performed. Actually, acid-free, buffered paper for book covers would be better.

## *Mold*

Mold is one of the more severe problems you will have to deal with after your books have gotten wet and stayed damp. That is why it is so important to take action as soon as possible after the unfortunate disaster. Once your papers become infested, it will be hard to get rid of.

**If your papers are afflicted by a little mold or mildew on the surface:**

1. Get them dry as soon as possible (moldy items are high priority!). This stuff grows fast!

2. Protect yourself with a face mask with a carbon filter (mold spores are very small and may penetrate regular dust masks). Some people are allergic to mold.

3. Outside, away from other papers, photos etc, remove the surface mold with a very soft, clean brush or..

4. Brush the mold into the nozzle of your vacuum cleaner and be sure to clean the brush off well after you are done so you don't transfer mold to another item later.

♦ Don't let the mold dust get on anything else or later, when the humidity rises, the mold spores that have settled will grow again.

5. If there is a residue on the surface of the paper, take a cotton swab and wipe the surface with isopropyl alcohol. This should remove the mold and may even kill some of it.

Being "preservation minded" means to get it dry, stop the mold, store it properly, handle it safely. These are what I want to teach you.

The emphasis is not on fixing rips, taking out stains, replacing missing pieces. This would be "restoration" and is not the purpose of this book. Besides, it would only slow you down in your efforts to save your family history.

The more severe the problem the more you will need professional help. The older the photo, the more urgently you will need a specialized professional.

### *Freezing stops mold in its tracks*

**If you have a couple of wet books to dry but can't get to it right away, then freeze the books in a freezer bag:**

- Separate several books in the same freezer bag with a piece of wax paper between each book.

- If you have numerous wet books, separate them with wax paper or freezer paper and pack them somewhat tight, spine down, in a wet proof container (Plastic garbage bag lined box, milk crate... something strong. They will be heavy).

- Freeze them right away.

- Don't let them sit around.

Call around town. Freeze drying may be an option. Look under "Freeze Drying" in the Yellow Pages.

### *Cleaning Dirty Books*

**Do not, under any circumstances, use:**

- Bleaches

- Detergents

- Fungicides

- Disinfectants

- Staples or paper clips on wet paper

- Colored paper to cover working surfaces, wipe up a mess or cover a book. The colors will bleed.

**For books that have a little mud on them and are not soaked:**

1. You can let the dirt dry...

2. Keep the book closed...

3. Then brush the dried mud off with a soft brush.

Courtesy Conservation Materials, Ltd.

Protect yourself from toxic materials (and problems with allergies):

* Gloves
* Dust masks

**or:**

1. Try and lift the mud off with a paper towel or rag.

2. Use a spray bottle for close range spraying and rinsing of mud away.

3. Blot up with clean towels as much water as possible.

4. Keep the book closed.

5. Follow directions for drying outlined earlier in the chapter.

6. Keep the cool air circulating to avoid mold.

**For books that are seriously wet and muddy:**

1. Gently rinse with clean cold water (Don't use warm water. It will dissolve the glues holding the book together).

2. If you are very careful, a very soft brush can be used to help get the mud off more completely (1" - 4" natural bristle paint brush will work fine. Some of the synthetic bristles are too stiff.) but don't try to rub or scrub. Be careful. Even this could cause damage.

3. Blot up with clean towels as much water as possible.

4. Once clean, follow the drying or freezing instructions outlined earlier in the chapter.

♦ It is possible that if you leave the mud on the book, once dry, you can just flake it off... However, letting mud dry on leather, paper and photographs will often result in a stain.

♦ Don't open or close the wet book while you are doing all of this.

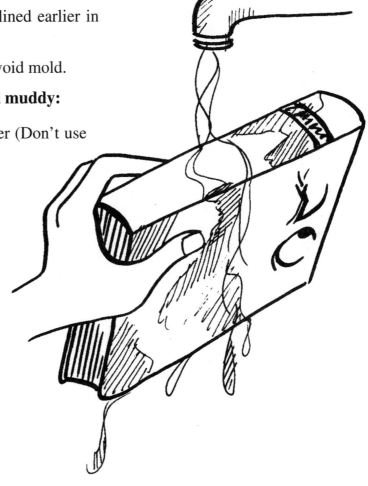

*Using a vacuum...*

### *Books which have dirt (dried) and dust:*

Dirty paper may not be an emergency situation. It won't get worse, especially if it is in a page protector. So cleaning, like rip repair, would be a second or third priority thing to do after everything else is saved from the disaster and safe.

**Do not, under any circumstances, use:**

♦ Bleaches

♦ Detergents

♦ Fungicides

♦ Disinfectants

♦ Staples or paper clips on wet paper

Before cleaning, make sure the paper is very dry.
Wash your hands before handling papers and keep them clean during the cleaning process by washing and thoroughly drying.

♦ Dust the book off with a clean soft dry 1" - 4" wide paint brush (I prefer the natural bristles to the synthetics).

♦ A vacuum cleaner can be used if screening material or netting is used between the book and the nozzle. Or use the brush nozzle on the vacuum cleaner or screen taped over the nozzle works great too.

♦ You should do this work outside so as not to put dust into the air which will redeposit on your clean books.

♦ Wear a dust mask. Besides the dirt and dust, some of the debris from earthquakes and construction can contain fiberglass, asbestos, and other toxic materials used in construction materials (you will not see them lying around).

**For more stubborn dirt:**

1. Clear a flat, clean work area.

2. Use an architectural eraser sack, or crumbled eraser.

3. Sprinkle a little on the surface and massage the paper's surface.

4. Do not rub vigorously. Do not insist in areas of pencil writing or drawing.

5. You will notice the color of the eraser material changing darker as it picks up dirt.

6. Brush off the eraser and dust with a very soft brush (1" - 4" natural bristle paint brush, very clean or new, will work fine).

7. Or vacuum up the eraser and dust through a clean window screen laid over the paper item with a brush tipped vacuum nozzle.

*Courtesy Conservation Materials, Ltd.*

Using an architectural pad or crumbled eraser...

A solid eraser (vs. the crumbled eraser) is also often used but there is a greater risk of crunching or wrinkling (damaging) the paper.

**If you are going to use a solid eraser:**

♦ Buy a vinyl eraser, not a rubber one.

♦ Don't rub vigorously.

♦ It's easy to abrade the paper (that's bad).

♦ Rub from the center of the paper towards the edge.

♦ Vacuum up the eraser stuff through a clean window screen laid over the paper item with a brush tipped vacuum nozzle or brush off with a soft brush.

♦ Pencil marks come off faster with solid erasers... be careful.

Courtesy Conservation Materials, Ltd.

Using a Groomstick...

Another interesting cleaning material is called a Groomstick. It isn't an eraser but instead, kind of absorbs up the dirt. It's soft and can be rubbed on or rolled over the surface without the risk of abrading the paper. You can still crunch or wrinkle the paper though so be careful. One of the nice things about the Groomstick is that it doesn't leave behind a residue nor is there anything to wipe off or vacuum up.

### Fire Damage

Books that have been in a fire can be cleaned with the same techniques as the dusty dirty books as described in the last chapter.

**If your books have that burnt smell do the following:**

1. Get a flat plastic container with a lid that seals that is larger than your book.

2. Cover the bottom of the container evenly with about 2" of charcoal briquettes (no additives like hickory flavoring or self lighting).

3. Over the charcoal, place a cookie rack.

4. Carefully place your smelly book on the rack. Don't get soot on it!

5. Seal it in (if the lid doesn't seal, use packing tape). Keep it in a cool spot for about 4 days.

6. Open it up and, voilá... no smell.

7. If you do get soot on your book, try using the crumbled eraser or Groomstick to get it clean again.

## After Your Book Has Cleaned Up

After all your worries and effort, don't just leave your book lying around. Don't toss it into a cardboard box and put it back on the garage floor. Look through the catalogs of the suppliers and see what appeals to you. There are some inexpensive ways to protect your books in the future:

♦ Store books in acid-free buffered boxes or plastic boxes (plastic milk crates).

♦ Buy a roll of 3 mil Mylar and cover your more important books.

♦ Don't store your important books mixed in with your run of the mill books. Avoid basements, attics, the barn or garage (if it leaks) and away from water storage tanks (like a water heater)

Acids (the wrong pH) cause paper to change color (yellow or brown), become brittle, "grow" spots called "foxing" and, generally speaking, to deteriorate quickly.

When thinking about covers for books and boxes for storage: Acid-free means that the acids have been neutralized or removed. But it doesn't mean the acids can't show up in the future. In fact, they probably will.

Buffered means that there is a time release cold capsule inside the paper that releases acid busters when they are needed. Therefore, the paper stays acid-free and safe.

## *Supply Locator: Books*

| **Supply** | **Number or Other Resouce** |
|---|---|
| | (Numbers correspond to vendor number on next page.) |
| Bags, plastic garbage | Supermarket |
| Book covers, acid free, buffered | 1, 3, 7, 8 |
| Bottles, spray | 1, 3, 7, 8, 12, Hardware store |
| Boxes, plastic | Supermarket, Drug store, Warehouse store |
| Boxes, book | 1, 3, 5, 6, 7, 8, 10, 12 |
| Brushes, soft, natural bristles | 1, 3, 7, 8, 12, Paint store |
| Charcoal briquettes | Supermarket |
| Crates, milk, plastic | Home Improvement |
| Dehumidifier | 6, Home Improvement |
| Erasers, draft gum cleaning | 1, 2, 3, 8, 12, Art store |
| Erasers, pads | 1, 3, 7, 8, Art store |
| Erasers, soft gum | 1, 3, 8, Art store, Office Supply |
| Fans | Home Improvement, Warehouse store |
| Hardware, anchor bolts, clasps, hooks, screws | 1, 2, 8, Hardware store |
| Leather reviver, collagen based | 1, 3, 8 |
| Mask, dust particle | 1, 2, 3, 7, 8, Hardware store |
| Mask, with carbon filter | 1, 3, 7, 8, Hardware store |
| Paper, freezer | Supermarket |
| Paper, wax | Supermarket |
| Quake Wax | 1, 7, 8 |
| Screen, window | Hardware store |
| Towels, white paper (no design or color) | Supermarket |
| Wax, caranuba | 1, 3, 8, Auto supply, Hardware store |

# SUPPLIERS OF PRESERVATION MATERIALS

**When you cannot find what you need at the local store, here is a list of suppliers who will have the hard to find stuff. Call the #800 and ask for a free catalog. They are usually very informative. Also, the lists of materials mentioned from each chapter have numbers that match with the suppliers on this page, so you know who sells what.**

**1.** Conservation Materials Ltd.
Box 2884, Sparks, NV 89431
Phone Toll Free (800) 733-5283
Phone (702) 331-0582
Fax (702) 331-0588
General preservation supplies. Has Collector Care Kits, scrapbooks and photo albums.

**2.** United Mfrs. Supplies, Inc.
80 Gordon Drive, Syosset, NY 11791
Phone Toll Free (800) 645-7260
Fax: (516) 496-7968
Hardware

**3.** Gaylord Archival Preservation & Conservation Supplies and Equipment
Box 4901, Syracuse, NY 13221
Phone Toll Free (800) 448-6160
Fax: (800) 272-3412
General preservation supplies.

**4.** Vue-All Inc.
P.O. Box 1994, Ocala, FL 32678
Phone (904) 732-3188
Phone Toll Free (800) 874-9737
Fax: (904) 867-8243
Specializes in good quality photo sleeves and pages

**5.** Metal Edge West, Inc.
2721 East 45th St., L.A., CA 90058
Phone (213) 588-2228
Phone Toll Free (800) 862-2228
Fax: (213) 588-2150
Internet http://www.eden.com:8080/~midnight/avi/shoppe1.avi
General preservation supplies.

**6.** Light Impressions
439 Monroe Avenue, Rochester, NY 14607-3717
Phone (716) 271-8960
Phone Toll Free (800) 828-6216
Fax: (800) 828-5539
General preservation supplies, scrapbooks and photo albums.

**7.** University Products, Inc.
P.O. Box 101, Holyoke, MA 01041
Phone (413) 532-3372
Phone Toll Free (800) 628-1912
Fax (800) 532- 9281
General preservation supplies, scrapbooks and photo albums.

**8.** Conservation Support Systems
P.O. Box 91746 Santa Barbara, CA 93190
Phone (805) 682-9843
Phone Toll Free (800) 482-6299
Fax: (805) 682-2064
General preservation supplies.

**9.** Bradley's Plastic Bag Co.
9130 Firestone Blvd. Downey, CA 90241
Phone (213) 923-5556
Phone (818) 289-0811
Phone Toll Free (800) 621-7864
Fax: (310) 862-4474
Plastic supplies of all kinds.

**10.** Archival Products
P.O. Box 1413, Des Moines, IA 50305
Phone Toll Free (800) 247-5323
Fax: (515) 262-6013
General preservation supplies.

**11.** Talas
213 W. 35th St., New York, NY 10001-1996
Phone (212) 219-0770
Fax: (212) 219-0735
General preservation supplies. Specializes in textile supplies.

**12.** Conservation Resources
800-H Forbes Place, Springfield, VA 22151
Phone Toll Free (800) 634-6932
Fax: (703) 321-0629
General preservation supplies.

# CHAPTER 6

## Art on paper: Watercolors, Pastels, Prints on Glossy Paper

*Before a disaster occurs:*

These items are going to be the most easily damaged when disaster hits. Your foresight in protecting them will make a huge difference in their preservation.

**The most common everyday (non disaster related) problems that can ruin these types of items are:**

♦ Too much light (causing fading, and yellowing of the paper).

♦ Careless handling (causing smudges, rips/tears, and scratches).

♦ Bad framing (causing acid burns, trimmed edges, stains from tape).

All of these problems can severely compromise the value (investment quality), damage the historical value or simply damage items that are important to you which could have otherwise gone undamaged. Once you finally notice they are damaged, they will already be pretty far gone. So, try and make yourself do something to preserve these items even if they don't look bad. (In this case the saying," If it ain't broke, don't fix it." is not a good rule of thumb.) A few guidelines will help you avoid these problems:

The dark stains on the upper corners are from contact cement. The stains couldn't be removed and diminished the value.

## Fading:

In short, don't put anything up on the wall and in the light that is important to you. (How about framing a copy? See the section on "Copywork.) The light doesn't have to be direct sunlight in order to fade. Fluorescent lights cause fading in rooms where no sunlight exists at all. Some items will fade faster than others.

**Some of the most sensitive are:**

♦ Signatures and writing in ballpoint pen are the most sensitive.

♦ Writing inks in general.

♦ Watercolors.

♦ Many color prints will change color, especially under fluorescent lights.

*Glass does not filter out ultraviolet light.*

Glass does not filter out ultraviolet light (which causes fading). There are types of glass or acrylic "glass" that reduce the amount of fading but do not eliminate it (UF3 Plexiglas, Museum Glass, True Vue; see your framer or plexi supplier). Window tinting can be purchased with a UV filter: this helps.

*Color photography that changes color is not fading because of light.*

Color photography that changes color is not fading because of light. The chemistry of the print is unstable and it will continue to change even in the dark. To preserve a photo that is changing color, take a new picture of your old picture (before the color goes too far out of whack) and make a new print. If this sounds like Greek to you, call a color photo lab under the Photography heading, in the yellow pages and ask for help.

*Do not do this for pastels, chalk drawings or anything that smudges.*

## Careless handling:

The following instructions apply to all art on paper except powdery pastels. Place your pastel artwork into a specialty box (see "Suppliers") or frame it with at least 1/4" space between glass and pastel ( or 1/2" space if using plexiglass because it sets up an electrostatic charge and will pull the pastel off the paper). Most importantly, do not let anything rub against the surface.

**Here are some very effective suggestions for protecting paper items:**

♦ Place your watercolors, engravings and art prints in storage using acid-free buffered storage materials or in the correct kind of plastic materials. An easy and fast way to protect your items is to use special envelopes like "L"velopes or you can put them into acid-free buffered manila envelopes. Or you can make custom envelopes out of Mylar sheets (encapsulation). Also, many items can be put into a single box with acid-free buffered separating sheets. Call the "Suppliers" and consult their catalogs for ideas.

♦ For those items that will fit, place important artwork on paper in page protectors. The 8 1/2" X 11" pages that I am recommending are clear plastic and you slide the letter in from the top or side. Page protectors come divided into sections so you can store several, say baseball cards, to a page. You can even economize by putting things in the sleeves back to back, however if you do this, you can't read anything that's written on the back. Some of the companies in the "Suppliers" section carry them. I have also bought them every once in awhile at the large warehouses like Price/Costco. Inquire around. You may be able to get them at stores like Fedco or Walmart.

♦ Place page protectors in a notebook. Any school notebook with a plastic cover will do for keeping the page protectors even though the notebook is not archival quality. (The colors of the cloth covered notebooks will run all over everything if it gets wet.) The papers are safe in their protective pages and the notebook won't hurt them. Be sure to label the notebook.

The correct quality of plastic used for storage should be polyester, polypropylene or polyethylene. Bad materials to be avoided are polyvinylchloride (PVC), vinyl or anything that smells weird or strong.

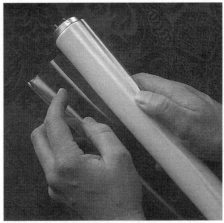
Courtesy Gaylord Bros.

Sleeves which filter out harmful uv rays (which cause fading) are easy to install by anyone.

Don't put anything up on the wall and in the light that is important to you.

The correct quality of plastic used for storage should be polyester, polypropylene or polyethylene. Bad materials to be avoided are polyvinylchloride (PVC), vinyl or anything that smells weird or strong.

Acids (the wrong pH) cause paper to change color (yellow or brown), become brittle, "grow" spots called "foxing" and, generally speaking, to deteriorate quickly.

When buying mat boards and archival papers, remember:

Acid-free means that the acids have been neutralized or removed. But it doesn't mean the acids can't show up in the future. In fact, they probably will.

Buffered means that there is a time release cold capsule inside the paper that releases acid busters when they are needed. Therefore, the paper stays acid-free and safe.

Mr. Acid Free Buffered: Protecting the weak and defenseless!

Also, don't worry at this point about the rips, stains, folds, etc. While doing this disaster prevention stuff, it is not the time to work on them. Get though the job of protecting your things as quickly and as thoroughly as possible.

**By taking these steps to separate and safeguard your art on paper, you have made sure that they will not:**

- ♦ Cause each other to yellow because of acids.
- ♦ Stick together if it gets humid.
- ♦ Run colors or inks together if they get wet.
- ♦ Get smudged, wrinkled, bent or torn when being handled.

The improvement in your storage will especially be good for your most fragile and beat up papers. But you will need to judge which papers can stand up in a notebook with a page protector and which ones should lie prone in an archival box.

**If you are going to put your paper items into storage (you won't be getting them out very often to look through them), I suggest the following:**

- ♦ Get a large plastic (polyethylene) container (like Rubbermaid or Tupperware).
- ♦ Put items already protected by acid-free folders or archival page protectors inside.
- ♦ You can place a silverfish tab inside to make it less hospitable for bugs. Put the tabs in a small glass or plastic jar with holes in the lid in order to make sure the pesticide doesn't touch the artwork.
- ♦ Use container's cover/lid to help keep out varmints and water, but
- ♦ Don't tape them shut to make them air tight. If you seal these items inside an airtight container, condensation inside on a hot muggy day will really cause some problems with mold and staining.

♦ Heavy duty plastic containers will fare better in an earthquake.

♦ I suggest not putting them in the attic.  Keep them in a cool dry place.

Another big plus is that, in the event of a disaster which involves water, you will have the papers stored in a clean manner.  Cardboard boxes and the like not only soak up water but the cardboard itself will bleed off impurities when wet and the yellowing will be carried by the water to stain everything thing else around.  Your fore-sight will keep this from happening.

I recommend photocopying (use color photocopy machine for best details) everything that's impor-tant and keep a copy at someone else's home.  These will be invaluable if you have an insurance claim in the future.

Photographs of individual valuable items and/or a video will be of great help when you have to file an insurance claim.  It will also help to put back together badly broken items.  Keep a copy at another location.

*Cool, dry storage suggestions: Inside an empty piece of furniture, in a pantry, under a bed, in the hard to reach areas of your kitchen cupboards.*

## *After a disaster occurs:*

An earthquake may crush everything around you but chances are you will not have great damage to your paper items (compared to your house or furniture).  Getting them cleaned off and into proper storage conditions are about the only things you need to do.  Even if you don't get them dusted off and into page protectors, they will still wait for you to get around to it.  Floods and water damage are another thing.  Let's talk about what to do after an earthquakes first:

Be careful when digging out of the rubble. You may dam-age more things during this work than was caused by the earthquake.

**The first thing you will want to do after you have pulled your watercolors etc. (and the broken frames) out, is:**

♦ Put them into something safe for protection. Look over the discussion on page protectors earlier in this chapter.

♦ Clean up broken glass from framing. Watch out for nails sticking out from broken frames. These sharp edges will cut and poke other art and furniture as you move things around. It is better to pull the nails or throw the frame away (if it isn't any good) so they don't damage anything. Check with your local framer, however, to see if your frame is worth repairing. Show your damaged antique frames to a local picture or antique dealer to see if you should save it.

♦ Dirty and dusty works or art will need to be cleaned.

♦ The final resting place should be in proper archival storage or properly framed.

### *Cleaning Dirty Paper*

Dirty paper may not be an emergency situation in and of itself. It won't get worse, especially if it is in a page protector. So, first take care of other, more urgent things, like wet paper, or broken items that could cut or break even worse. Cleaning your dusty and dirty (I'm talking about dry dirt, not muddy dirt) things would be a second or third priority thing to do.

While handling a lot of different pages, it is important to wear gloves so as not to transfer the dirt from page to page. Recommended gloves for this use are polyethylene surgical gloves or white cotton gloves (to be bought at medical supply stores or conservation supply houses).

*Don't ever use newsprint or butcher paper when storing paper items.*

**Once everything else is saved from the disaster and safe and you are ready to clean your works of art on paper, do not, under any circumstances, use:**

- ◆ Water
- ◆ Bleaches
- ◆ Detergents
- ◆ Disinfectants

**Here is how to proceed (Do not do this on pastels, charcoal or chalk):**

1. Clear a flat, clean work area.

2. Put clean paper down (unprinted newsprint or butcher paper is fine) but don't ever use these two kinds of paper when storing items.

3. Use an architectural eraser sack, or crumbled eraser. Sprinkle a little on the surface and massage the paper's surface.

- ◆ Do not rub vigorously.  Do not insist in areas of pencil writing or drawing.  Erase from the center area towards the edge of the paper.

- ◆ You will notice the color of the eraser material changing darker as it picks up dirt.

4. Brush off the eraser and dust with a very soft brush (A 1" - 4" natural bristle paint brush, very clean or new,  will work fine).

- ◆ Or vacuum up the eraser and dust through a clean window screen laid over the paper item with a brush tipped vacuum nozzle.

5. Put into archival quality page protectors or other archival holder.

A solid eraser (vs. the crumbled eraser) is also often used but there is a greater risk of crunching or wrinkling (damaging) the paper.

Courtesy Conservation Materials, Ltd.

Using an architectural pad or crumbled eraser...

Courtesy  Conservation Materials, Ltd.

Using a Groomstick...

**If you are going to use a solid eraser:**

1. Buy a vinyl eraser, not a rubber one.

2. Don't rub vigorously.

3. Its easy to abrade the paper (that's bad).

4. Rub from the center of the paper towards the edge.

5. Pencil marks come off faster with solid erasers... Be careful.

6. Put into archival quality page protectors or other archival holder.

Another interesting cleaning material is called a Groomstick. It isn't an erasure but instead, kind of absorbs up the dirt. It's soft and can be rubbed on or rolled over the surface without the risk of abrading the paper. You can still crunch or wrinkle the paper though so be careful. One of the nice things about the Groomstick is that it doesn't leave behind a residue nor is there anything to wipe off or vacuum up.

These types of treatments, when cautiously performed will be good for use on watercolors and prints of all kinds in color and black and white. Do not use these techniques on pastels, charcoal or chalk (you will rub them off the paper).

**Cleaning pastels, charcoal or chalk drawings:**

♦ Take your artwork to a specialized conservator.

Do not rub on wet paper. Do not rub on the paint or image area. You will quickly damage the color or drawing.

**DO NOT TRY:**

♦ Rubbing on it with a rag (you will rub it off and it will look bad).

♦ Using water (it will stain and turn ugly in the blink of an eye).

♦ Use any household cleaning materials (they will

stain and turn ugly in the blink of an eye and they will leave harmful substances in the artwork when it dries).

♦ Do not use a fixative on the artwork. It causes the powdery colors to shrink in on themselves and look anemic. If the artwork is dirty and you use a fixative, you will seal the dirt into the artwork.

## *Ripped paper:*

Dry, torn paper really isn't an "emergency." It won't grow mold or get worse if you are careful. You can always fix it later when the emergency situation passes. In the mean time you can protect torn and damaged papers with archival quality plastic page protectors, acid-free buffered paper folders or something similar.

## Repairing rips:

If you are losing sleep over ripped artwork, the following procedure may help you relax. The steps to be taken will need to be applied more delicately if the ripped paper is thin. Or you may have to repeat some steps if the paper is thick and stiff.

*Don't ever use newsprint or butcher paper when storing paper items.*

1. Clear a flat, clean work area.

2. Put clean paper down (unprinted newsprint or butcher paper is fine) but don't ever use these two kinds of paper when storing items.

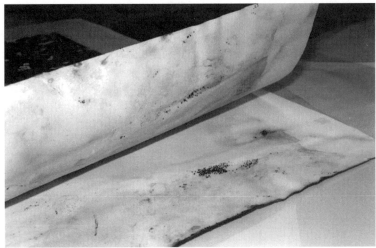

3. Take a DAMP cotton swab (distilled water) and, along the back side.

4. Roll the swab along the fold, crease or distortion.  Be careful not to roll up the edge of the paper (fibers) on the cotton swab. Do not rub on wet paper. Do not rub on the paint or image area. You will quickly damage the color or drawing.

*Don't let papers lie together when wet.  Mold will grow and stain the paper.*

5. Do not saturate the paper, but instead apply only light humidity on the wrinkled area.

6. Place the dampened paper between sheets of absorbent paper toweling and...

7. As a weight, put a book on top (with wax paper between the paper towel and the book) to let the page dry under pressure. See directions for drying in chapter on "Paper."

8. Once the page has been dried and the edges have been realigned, then a reversible archival document repair tape can be used on the back side for local temporary repair. See sections on "Where to Buy" and "Suppliers" and follow the directions on box.

9. DO NOT USE AN OFF THE SHELF TAPE FROM YOUR LOCAL STORE !!!!!!!!!!!!!

10. Put your repaired item into a page protector or appropriate envelope/holder.

11. Get a good nights sleep.

**If your artwork on paper has gotten wet:**

*... you don't have time to just let them sit.*

Action must be taken within 72 hours or mold will begin to grow, maybe sooner.

1. Get the water to stop (as if you needed to to be told that!).

2. Go over building and personal safety checklists (see lists in Appendix).

3. Get fresh circulating air (open a window and turn on a couple of fans into the room as soon as possible (call a rental company for a commercial dehumidifier).

*See section on handling and drying wet frames in chapter on Frames.*

4. Do not turn on the heat.

**Remove all framed items from their frames. This is easier said than done:**

1. Set aside a clean flat area to work.

2. Put down a layer of butcher paper or unprinted newsprint (newspaper ink can rub off onto the items your working on). But if you are working with frames and newsprint is all you have, go ahead and use it.

3. Put the frame face down onto the paper.

4. Remove and throw away all the nails, tape, clamps etc. on the back side that hold the artwork into the frame (you will be using new materials when you put it back together).

5. Remove the hanging hardware (wire and screw eyes) and throw them away. They are dirty and possibly rusty which will rub off onto other items (you will be using new materials when you put it back together).

6. VERY CAREFULLY lift the backing board off. Watch out! The artwork may be attached to it. If so, lift the backing board, artwork and the front mat all out together. If it is not attached to anything, throw it away (you may want to keep it if it has important writing on it).

7. Lift the artwork out with the backing board and front window mat. If the front window mat is not attached to the artwork, throw it away. If the mat is nicely decorated or historical, you may want to have it duplicated when you do the new framing. Dry it out in the open air, separate from the artwork. The mat board doesn't have to look great when it's dry... just good enough for the framer to have it copied.

8. Once the artwork has had all detached mat boards and backing boards discarded, cut the flaps (hinges) holding the artwork to the backing board so the artwork will come free. If the artwork and the mat boards are all stuck together in a mess, take everything to a conservator.

9. Throw away all broken glass, protruding nails and ugly damaged frames. Something else is bound to get damaged if these things lay around awhile.

Be very careful. Wet mat board will fall apart and the glues on some tapes holding the mats together and the artwork in it's place can give away.

* If you try to pull apart papers that are glued together you will pull the paper apart.
* If you try to remove tape off of wet paper, you will pull the paper apart.
* Wet paper rips very easily.

The best choice for a paper towel would be the thickest towel possible that holds together when wet and has the least amount of texture to it. Pick the towel that is as lint-free as possible and if possible, plain white (no bunnies, flowers, or hearts).

The dark rectangle around the image is the acid burn from the window mat. This engraving by Edward Borein also has a bad case of mold stains. Yellowing of the paper and embrittle-ment are due to acids. A professional conservator can make this look great. You won't be able to fix any of these problems, but you can preserve and protect it for the future.

Be careful your "drying area" is not also the "dog area" or the "kids area."

Now that you have the artwork freed from the framing, proceed with the drying instructions.

**If you have loose papers in water:**

1. Begin salvage efforts by getting small piles of papers out of the water.

2. But don't try to lift large wet paper items out of drawers or from the water. They will rip to shreds.

3. Sponge out the water first.

4. Let the large items dry (circulating air) in the drawer.

Wet paper falls apart easily. If you must handle a sheet of wet paper, a good suggestion is to get a sheet of good strong paper towel and lay the wet piece of paper on the paper toweling and move both of the sheets together. The best choice for a paper towel would be the thickest towel possible that holds together when wet and has the least amount of texture to it. Pick the towel that is as lint-free as possible and if possible, plain white (no bunnies, flowers, or hearts).

### *How to dry wet papers*

**Do not, under any circumstances, use:**

- ◆ Bleaches
- ◆ Detergents
- ◆ Fungicides
- ◆ Disinfectants
- ◆ Staples or paper clips on wet paper
- ◆ Do not pull off tapes used for framing or repair when the paper is wet.

**If you don't have too many to dry:**

1. In a well ventilated area you can lay each individual paper out on a dry clean surface to air dry. Be careful that breezes, wind, kids etc. don't blow them around.

**If you have numerous items to dry:**

1. Do not rub, clean, or try to fix papers while they are wet.

2. If you feel particularly skilled with your hands, you may want to try to carefully align the edges of a rip the paper before putting artwork between paper toweling and under books to dry.  A small blade (pocket knife?) or flat utensil (palette knife) will be helpful  when trying to move the delicate paper fibers into place.

3. A piece of wet or damp paper can be dried between sheets of paper toweling by putting one or two sheets of absorbent paper towels (no colors, no texture, no perfumes) on each side of the wet piece of paper to be dried (be sure there are no folds in the art work or in the paper towels or the folds will be made permanent once the whole is put under pressure to dry).

4. Place a clean board (possibly a kitchen cutting board) or a book on top as a weight. If you use a book, it should be larger than the item being dried.

*Very Important:*

♦ Place a sheet of wax paper, or plastic between the book and the paper towels so the books don't absorb the water.

♦ Don't put too much weight on the artwork or you will transfer the color of the watercolor, gouache and many kinds of drawings onto the paper toweling.  Just the cutting board or just one thick book should be enough.

If you happen to miss exchanging the paper towels because you were busy, or you let it sit overnight, no problem. Exchange dry paper toweling for damp ones the first chance you get.

♦ Let the "artwork sandwich" sit for about an hour before exchanging the damp or wet paper towel for a dry one. Change both the top towel and the bottom one. Do this again, two or three times, at four hour shifts.

♦ Once the paper towels have absorbed water from the artwork being dried, they can be set aside to dry and can be reused later (dry them in another area so as not to add moisture to the air). Once the paper towels begin to get dirty and collect stains from the artwork that are being dried, they can be thrown away.

The drying cycle of exchanging dry paper towels for wet ones should be repeated for at least a couple of days until the papers are dry. If you take the papers out from under the book/weights before they are perfectly dry, then they will distort or warp.

Once again, it is important to keep cool air circulating and to dry them out as soon as possible in order to keep mold growth at a minimum.

### Can't treat it? Freeze it!

If a large quantity of papers have become wet and drying them out immediately is not possible, then place them in a large plastic container (Tupperware, plastic milk crates) or in the large freezer bags and put the piles of paper in a freezer (rent space in a commercial freezer if you are really in trouble) within 48 hours. They will wait there patiently until they can be treated.

♦ Piles of paper should be separated with a sheet of wax paper as you put them into boxes or bags.

♦ Don't try and separate each individual sheet as the handling of single wet sheets of paper can be very difficult!

♦ Handle with care!

♦ Check local commercial services for freeze drying.

As I stated at the beginning of this chapter, art on paper doesn't survive a disasters like floods very well. But if you are careful, you can make a difference in it's preservation if there is an earthquake.

"Acts of God," as the insurance company puts it, are not the only disasters we know. A grandchild knocking a cherished watercolor by Grandpa off the wall can be alarming. A beautiful pastel whose frame and glass were broken during shipment can send shivers up your neck.

Don't be afraid to call a professional conservator for advice. Try calling a paper conservator and you may find one that works on painted art work. Or call a painting or fine art conservator and you may find one that works on paper items. Stay away from restorers who work on everything under the sun and framers who fix things too. This is very good advice... it will save you money and maybe save your artwork from being ruined.

***Good luck!***

Papers that have yellowed are showing advanced stages of deterioration.  A paper conservator can remove the acids & stains and give it new life.

## *Supply Locator: Art on paper: Watercolors, Pastels, Prints on Glossy Paper*

| **Supply** | **Number or Other Resouce** |
|---|---|
| | (Numbers correspond to vendor number on next page.) |
| Bags, freezer | 6, 7, Supermarket |
| Bags, plastic | 1, 2, 3, 6, 7, 8 |
| Boxes, archival | 1, 3, 5, 6, 7, 8, 10, 12 |
| Boxes, specialty (Rubbermaid, Tupperware) | Supermarket, Drug store, Warehouse store |
| Brush, natural bristle paint | 1, 3, 7, 8, 12, Paint store |
| Crates, milk, plastic | 3, Home Improvement |
| Dehumidifier | 6, Home Improvement Warehouse store |
| Encapsulation, mylar sheets | 1, 3, 5, 6, 7, 8, 12 |
| Envelopes, acid free manila | 1, 3, 5, 6, 7, 8, 12 |
| Envelopes, "L"velope | 1, 2, 3, 5, 6, 7, 8, 12 |
| Erasers, architectural eraser sack | 1, 3, 7, 8, 12, Art store |
| Erasers, crumbled | 1, 3, 8, Art store |
| Erasers, soft gum | 1, 2, 3, 8, Art store, Office Supply |
| Erasers, solid vinyl | 1, 3, Art store, Office Supply |
| Fans, electric | Hardware or Warehouse store |
| Folders, acid free | 1, 2, 3, 5, 6, 7, 8, 10, 12 |
| Glass, museum | 1, 3, 8, Glass store, Frame shop |
| Glass, True Vue | 8, Glass store, Frame shop |
| Glass, UV filter window tinting | 1, 3, 7, see Yellow Pages |
| Gloves, polyethylene surgical | 1, 3, 7, 8, Surgical supply |
| Gloves, white cotton | 1, 2, 3, 6, 7, 8, 12 |
| Groom stick | 1 |
| Knife, palette | 1, 3, 8, Art store |
| Mylar sheets | 1, 3, 5, 6, 7, 8, 12 |
| Notebooks, plastic school covered | 1, 3, Office Supply store Warehouse store |
| Page protectors, plastic | 1, 2, 3, 5, 6, 7, 8, 12 |
| Paper, butcher | 3, Paper Supply store |
| Paper, unprinted newsprint | 3, 7, 8, Paper Supply store |
| Paper, wax | Supermarket |
| Plexiglas | 1, 2, 3, 6, 8, Frame shop |
| Silverfish Tabs | Home Improvement |
| Storage materials, acid free buffered | 1, 3, 5, 6, 7, 8, 10 |
| Swabs, cotton | 1, 3, 8, Supermarket, Drug store |
| Tape, archival document repair | 1, 2, 3, 6, 7, 8, 12 |
| Towels, paper | Supermarket |
| Water, distilled | Supermarket |

# SUPPLIERS OF PRESERVATION MATERIALS

**When you cannot find what you need at the local store, here is a list of suppliers who will have the hard to find stuff. Call the #800 and ask for a free catalog. They are usually very informative. Also, the lists of materials mentioned from each chapter have numbers that match with the suppliers on this page, so you know who sells what.**

**1.** Conservation Materials Ltd.
Box 2884, Sparks, NV 89431
Phone Toll Free (800) 733-5283
Phone (702) 331-0582
Fax (702) 331-0588
General preservation supplies. Has Collector Care Kits, scrapbooks and photo albums.

**2.** United Mfrs. Supplies, Inc.
80 Gordon Drive, Syosset, NY 11791
Phone Toll Free (800) 645-7260
Fax: (516) 496-7968
Hardware

**3.** Gaylord Archival Preservation & Conservation Supplies and Equipment
Box 4901, Syracuse, NY 13221
Phone Toll Free (800) 448-6160
Fax: (800) 272-3412
General preservation supplies.

**4.** Vue-All Inc.
P.O. Box 1994, Ocala, FL 32678
Phone (904) 732-3188
Phone Toll Free (800) 874-9737
Fax: (904) 867-8243
Specializes in good quality photo sleeves and pages

**5.** Metal Edge West, Inc.
2721 East 45th St., L.A., CA 90058
Phone (213) 588-2228
Phone Toll Free (800) 862-2228
Fax: (213) 588-2150
Internet http://www.eden.com:8080/~midnight/avi/shoppe1.avi
General preservation supplies.

**6.** Light Impressions
439 Monroe Avenue, Rochester, NY 14607-3717
Phone (716) 271-8960
Phone Toll Free (800) 828-6216
Fax: (800) 828-5539
General preservation supplies, scrapbooks and photo albums.

**7.** University Products, Inc.
P.O. Box 101, Holyoke, MA 01041
Phone (413) 532-3372
Phone Toll Free (800) 628-1912
Fax (800) 532- 9281
General preservation supplies, scrapbooks and photo albums.

**8.** Conservation Support Systems
P.O. Box 91746 Santa Barbara, CA 93190
Phone (805) 682-9843
Phone Toll Free (800) 482-6299
Fax: (805) 682-2064
General preservation supplies.

**9.** Bradley's Plastic Bag Co.
9130 Firestone Blvd. Downey, CA 90241
Phone (213) 923-5556
Phone (818) 289-0811
Phone Toll Free (800) 621-7864
Fax: (310) 862-4474
Plastic supplies of all kinds.

**10.** Archival Products
P.O. Box 1413, Des Moines, IA 50305
Phone Toll Free (800) 247-5323
Fax: (515) 262-6013
General preservation supplies.

**11.** Talas
213 W. 35th St., New York, NY 10001-1996
Phone (212) 219-0770
Fax: (212) 219-0735
General preservation supplies. Specializes in textile supplies.

**12.** Conservation Resources
800-H Forbes Place, Springfield, VA 22151
Phone Toll Free (800) 634-6932
Fax: (703) 321-0629
General preservation supplies.

# CHAPTER 7

## Paintings

### Before a disaster occurs:

Damage due to careless handling is avoidable. Damage due to cleaning the artwork with Windex or 409 is avoidable (don't do it!). To avoid a disaster, both small and large, here are a few common sense suggestions:

Make sure all your hanging hooks, wire and eye holes are strong (not about to break or frayed) and well attached.

← Don't hang artwork in high traffic areas of the home or office.

← Don't hang artwork over heaters or fireplaces where they will get hot.

← Avoid direct sunlight.

← Don't put paintings in the game room (Frisbees and paintings are not compatible).

This pioneer portrait of artist C.C.A. Christiansen's wife was loaned for a pioneer celebration. It fell off a pioneer tripod onto a pioneer bed post. Don't lend old fragile keepsakes.

- Be aware that if you have taken your paintings and frames off the wall, that there are hooks, nails, wires, etc., on the back of the frame which may badly scratch or otherwise damage furniture or other paintings onto which these frames are leaned.

- Protect and remove all artwork from the room before moving furniture or painting. Boxes, cardboard, bubble wrap, tape etc. may be bought from a moving company or paper supply company.

**Properly hanging a painting will do much to ensure its safety:**

A couple of balls of Quake Wax in the two lower corners will keep your frames straight on the wall.

- Make sure the screw eyes and wire are in good shape (not frayed or loose). This will be important when the next earthquake hits. You can buy replacement materials from your local art store or see "Suppliers".

- Make sure the hanging hook (on the wall) is well anchored. In an earthquake a loose fitting hook will give away. When putting up an hanging hook, try to anchor the hook into a stud. If this is not possible, or if you are trying to hang something on a cement wall, buy the right kind of expanding sleeves for the screw (to be used in place of the nail) from the hardware store.

- Use a couple of balls of Quake Wax between the wall and the frame to hold the frame where you put it (so it doesn't keep going skeewampus) and it will also hold more securely in an earthquake. See "Where to Buy."

Photographs of individual valuable items and/or a video will be of great help when you have to file an insurance claim. It will also help to put back together badly broken items. Keep a copy of photographs and appraisals at another location.

## *After a disaster occurs:*

**DO NOT do the following!**

♦ Do not handle/ touch damaged areas.

♦ Do not brush dirt off or clean on flaking/ ripped areas.

♦ Do not put pressure on the front of the painting.

♦ Do not use any

> Cleaning solutions
> Detergents
> Fungicides
> Bleaches

♦ Do not put tape on the front of the painting.

♦ Do not hose off paintings or frames. Let the mud dry.

♦ Paintings should not be removed from their stretcher bars and rolled up.

♦ Do not attempt to glue rips back together or to touch up scratches:  you will not be able to do them satisfactorily and will increase the cost of proper conservation work later.  Should your painting be torn and if you are compelled to reinforce it in some way, tape may be temporarily applied to the back of the fabric to help hold the flaps in place.

### *Earthquakes*

After the upheaval of an event like an earthquake, much of the damage to paintings comes in the ensuing frantic activity of moving things around.  Leaning a painting against the sharp corner of a table or paintings leaning precariously against themselves against a wall where shifting may take place and a corner of a frame will go through another canvas are often more common and dangerous than the emergency situation itself. If your painting looks OK after the turmoil, or barely damaged, try some of the following suggestions:

♦ Dusting and surface cleaning can be done with a soft brush (a new (clean) paint brush with long bristles will be fine) and your vacuum cleaner. Brush the dust and dirt off the frame and artwork into the sucking end of the vacuum cleaner nozzle (put the brush nozzle on for added protection). This will keep the dirt from getting thrown into the air... which would only settle someplace else, right?

♦ Gather pieces of frames or chunks of artwork and put them in a baggie. Label the baggie and staple to the back of the frame or stretcher bars. Save it for a conservator to repair properly.

### Cleaning out the debris from behind the stretcher bars and the painting:

Before you bring the canvas taut on its stretcher bars you may want to remove debris from between the stretcher bars of an old painting and its canvas. Most of the dust, dirt and debris that has dropped inside behind the stretcher bar is located along the bottom of the painting. Work on a clean surface. This job is best done if your artwork is out of it's frame.

Tip painting forward so debris falls clear. Note padding on table.

1. Holding the painting by the edges, tip your painting up on the side with the back of the painting facing towards you.

2. Position it upside down and tip the top of the painting slightly towards you.

3. A very skinny (skewer stick, tooth pick or thin artist spatula) thin object can be moved behind the painting and the stretcher bar to dislodge any material.

4. Because you have it tipped forward, the debris will fall out on the table.

5. Be very careful about this procedure watching the front of the painting for bulges and being careful not to be too rough. Very careful persistence will yield good results.

6. Once you have dislodged the materials resting between the painting and the stretcher bars do not try and push down on the bulges that may be still showing on the surface on the painting. This will most likely cause flaking and paint loss.

### How to "Stretch" or Key Out Your Painting

Paintings shouldn't be "stretched"... they need to brought "taut" on their stretcher bars (the wooden frame that the artwork is mounted on)... I know, picky, picky, picky... anyway, we know what we mean, don't we?

**Before you get started, an inspection of the artwork is in order:**

♦ Is there flaking on the front of the painting? Don't risk losing any more! get this fixed first.

♦ Carefully inspect the edge of the painting where it wraps around the stretcher bars. Many times a painting shows wrinkling and deformations because the canvas has split at this edge. This is a problem that you should not take care of but for which you should seek professional assist-ance. If the canvas is split or shows signs of splitting, then expanding the stretcher bars to increase the tautness of the canvas will only rip out the edges of the painting more. If this is the case, you can do nothing to improve the tautness of the canvas. Your artwork is falling apart and needs to be looked at by a professional conservator.

Over the years I have found many interesting items between paintings and their mountings. On a large painting I once found an old chisel dating from the 1700's, I have found dead lizards, many different kinds of leaves and pine needles, I have found BB's and bullets along with small toys, seeds of all kinds and lots and lots of wooden keys (the wooden wedges that go in the corner of the stretcher bars).

Careful !
Old canvas can be brittle.

Wiping paintings down with a damp cloth can do serious damage after years. The small white dots on the right is where paint is flaking.

It's better to adjust the stretcher bars slowly in order to keep control over the tautness than rather trying to hit heavy blows and do it quickly.

♦ If the edge of a painting is not split or broken, then you can test to see how brittle the fabric is. Along the tacking edge (where the artwork is nailed or stapled to the wood) there is fabric which can be carefully taken between two fingers and split. If the fabric splits or breaks easily, then the fabric is very brittle. If however the fabric does not tear easily, the greater the strength of the fabric. Please note that the more brittle and deteriorated the fabric of the painting is the more danger there is to damage by ripping and by poking holes. You must be that much more careful due to the higher risk level.

♦ Are there bulges or gathers at the corners of the painting? If they are hard or stiff, they will be fragile and you need to be very careful not to try too hard to have they completely removed by expanding the stretcher bars.

♦ In the corners of the back side of the stretcher bars you need to notice two things:

1. Is the corner or angle of the wooden bars (where they meet) nailed or fastened together? And...

2. Are there wooden or plastic wedges in the corners?

If the corners are nailed or fastened shut, you can't expand the stretcher bars. Take the painting to a framer for help (he/she may not even charge you for the help). If you have the wooden wedges missing, you can't expand the stretcher bars either. A frame shop should be able to give you some free. Also, the art stores carry plastic keys and may give them to you free. You will need two wedges for each corner and one for each cross bar.

### Keying Out The Stretcher Bars

Turn the painting face down onto the covered work surface. Double check to see that there are no nails, wedges of wood or other debris on the table which would cause indentations, scrapes, or punctures in the surface of the painting. In a nutshell, we are going to hammer in the keys to force the corners of the stretcher bars to spread, thereby bring the painting taut. This is how to go about it:

1. Replace any missing keys.

2. It is important to protect the painting from wayward glances of the hammer. Protect the painting with a 4 or 5" by 4 or 5" piece of cardboard which can be slid neatly between the fabric and the stretcher bar. Do not force the board as you will damage the painting.

3. Once there is protection between the canvas and the stretcher bars, then the keys or wedges can be tapped into place with a hammer.

Technique: Use a small hammer. Big heavy hammers are harder to control. It is best to tap each key or wedge a little, making a rotation of the keys several times. The piece of cardboard should be moved to each corner as those keys are tapped out and the corners expanded. Notice the distortions as they are removed. If the painting is brittle, then you do not want to put a lot of stress on the painting. In fact, the painting will be better off if it is a little slack.

How much is enough? That depends on how fragile the painting is. Old brittle unreinforced paintings should be left a little slack. Paintings in better condition can be held a little tighter. By tapping the surface of the painting you will get a feeling of how tight it is stretched. If it sounds like a tambourine or a bongo, then it is stretched much too tight. Movement of the surface should be minimal.

### How to Remove Dents and Dings

If you have any dents, dings or dimples... any way you want to call them, feel lucky that your artwork wasn't brittle enough or wasn't hit hard enough to rip it (there's an optimistic side to everything!). A rip, you shouldn't mess with. A ding, I can help you with. Properly stretching a painting should remove the draws or uneven

Tap the wooden keys carefully. Place a piece of cardboard between keys and fabric.

As far as you are concerned, a little loose is better than too tight.

A good rule of thumb: If the looseness of the canvas doesn't come taut easily, don't force it.

stretching marks in the corners of the painting and should have removed bulges in other areas of the painting if they existed. After properly keying out the canvas do the following:

1. A dimple or local indentation can be carefully treated by putting the painting face down on a hard clean surface.

2. Under the area of the dimple or indentation it is best to put a piece of release paper (such as wax paper or silicone release papers) between the painting and your table. This process involves heat and the heat may soften the resin on the surface and attach your painting to the table unless precautions are otherwise taken.

3. With the painting face down on a clean surface with a release paper between the surface of the painting and the table top, take a cotton tipped applicator and dipping it in water, lightly moisten only the area of the indentation.

4. Now, once humidified, the indentation should be slightly warmed with the tip of an iron. No pressure should be exerted and the iron should not be put flat down on the painting. Carefully try to heat up only the area of the dent. Continue heating this area not allowing it to get hot.

5. Once warmed, you may see steam rise and you will see the spot begin to dry. Then reapply the heat, do this several times until the fabric is no longer damp and the dent has been removed.

6. Continue doing this procedure until the fabric is very dry.

7. The indentation will probably be removed immediately once humidity and heat are applied however if you do not dry out your fabric by continued applications of heat, you may cause damage to that area of the painting by allowing the fabric to shrink or allowing the distortion to return because of the wet fabric.

Courtesy Conservation Materials, Ltd.

If your damaged area of the painting corresponds to a spot opposite the stretcher bars (in other words, you can't get to the back of the painting) do not remove the painting from the stretcher bars. Consult with a professional conservator.

### *What to Do About Rips... Even Big Ugly Ones!*

The most important thing to do about a rip is to keep the paint from flaking. Unless your painting is very brittle and you are clumsy, the rip won't get worse... but you can continue to lose paint. The first aid emergency technique for stopping flaking is as follows:

*How to keep loose paint from flaking off.*

- ◆ Buy a small artist's painting brush ( size 3 - 6) from a supplier in this book or from your local art store.

- ◆ But a small (the smallest one they have... you will need very little depending on how much flaking you have to consolidate) bottle of liquid varnish. A synthetic varnish is best. "Soluvar" is a good brand, if you can find it. Do not use epoxies, urathanes, or white glues.

- ◆ On your clean work surface, lie the painting (it does not need to be out of its frame) down face up. This should be a well ventilated area.

- ◆ Light-handedly (you are not painting your house!) brush on the varnish, full strength, only on the areas that are flaking. Do not varnish the whole painting!

- ◆ If possible, do not get the varnish on the ends of the fabric's threads. No biggie if you do... but it would be nice if you didn't. The conservator that will later fix the ripped, frayed edges may appreciate it.

I can't tell you how many times people tell me about taking the painting down to paint and soon after, a chair leg goes through the painting. In this case, a penny's worth of cardboard (or mirror box) would have prevented many dollars worth of repair.

♦ Let dry an hour before moving the painting (or the varnish may drip).

♦ Allow to dry overnight before packing.

♦ Protect and preserve! Until you get the painting to a conservator it must be protected. Place a piece of toilet paper or paper towel on the areas that you treated with the varnish then sandwich the painting (and frame?) between two sheets of cardboard and tape closed. Additional padding for corners of ornate frames can be done with bubble wrap, foam or wadded up paper and tape. Another option is to get a "mirror box" from a moving company.

♦ Be sure to label, on the outside, what it is.

Remember, the more paint is knocked off in the damaged area, the more work will be needed to bring the painting into acceptable condition once again (the more it will cost to fix... the less it will be worth, yeh yeh yeh, blah blah blah).

### In Case of Flooding or Wet Paintings

**Here's your list of DO NOTs**

♦ Do not lay paintings out in the sun to dry. If you have numerous items to dry, set the paintings and frames on blocks, face up and get the air circulating.

♦ Don't use heaters (mold!).

♦ Don't touch the face of wet paintings.

♦ Do not handle/ touch damaged areas.

♦ Do not put pressure on the front of the painting.

♦ Do not use any:

        cleaning solutions
        detergents
        fungicides
        bleaches

- Do not hose off paintings or frames. Let the mud dry.

- Do not wrap wet or humid paintings.

- Do not put paintings in commercial freezers.

- Paintings should not be removed from their stretcher bars and rolled up.

**If a painting is wet:**

- Drain off all the water from the painting and frame (and from behind the stretcher bars) immediately. Blot away pooling water put don't put pressure on the painting!

- Get it dry as soon as possible (immediately). Put a fan blowing on or use a blow dryer directly on the back of the wet canvas but do not heat up the air or use a hot blow dryer.

- Set items out to dry in a separate room from the flooded area, if possible. They will dry quicker.

It is possible that the fabric (especially 19th century pictures) has shrunk causing what is called "tent cleavage", the buckling of the paint along tented ridges. If this has happened to your paintings, do not touch, do not attempt to fix, "do not pass go," "do not collect $200." Leave the painting in the prone position and contact a conservator as soon as possible. It may be possible for the professional to lie the paint back down onto the painting so that no damage will ever be apparent. However, if the flaked paint has been lost then the costs for proper treatment will soar and the value of the painting will plummet.

The most important thing that must be done is to keep the painting from flaking and the damaged areas from getting worse. In these few short paragraphs it is impossible to give adequate instruction for safe treatment of paintings; therefore, it is recommended that you call a quality, professional painting conservator immediately.

Detail of Portrait of Karl Maeser, used with permission of Museum of Art, Brigham Young University.

When paintings get wet, the fabric can shrink and the paint pops off.

Read the section on "Frames."

### About Cleaning Paintings

I know that you want to know how to clean your paintings. It is an often asked question. The problem is I can't tell you. It would make you dangerous. What works on one painting, will ruin another... or do absolutely nothing. Some of the conditions that can affect a cleaning are:

♦ The age of the painting,

♦ The amount of paint,

♦ Whether the paint was lean or loaded,

♦ Whether varnish was added to the painting medium,

♦ Whether the painting is in oil, acrylic, tempera, watercolor, gouache or a mixture (which is common).

♦ What is on the painting? House grime? Uncle Bob's special varnish mixture? Linseed oil varnish? Nicotine? Smoke from the fire place?

♦ How many times has it been "restored"?

♦ Then, of course, the present condition of the painting makes a big difference.

Of all the conservation treatments that are performed by professionals, cleaning is one of the most delicate and risky. Not only the right solvent mixture is required, but the techniques of applying those solvents and the talent of the conservator are very important. So, as you can see, there is no off the shelf solution that will properly and safely clean a painting. Some art historians have surmised that more paintings have been ruined and lost due to poor restorers and cleaning that due to all the volcanoes, earthquakes and floods put together!

It's not good for your paintings either.

The only thing I can recommend to you is to be careful when you wipe off the dust with a clean soft rag (watch out for flaking) or a feather duster (don't use a dust spray cleaner on the rag).  If you have a dirty painting and if you want it cleaned your safest option is to speak with a conservation professional who will help you to recognize the problems and give you an estimate for the work.  Please refer to the chapter on choosing a conservator.

## *How to Pack Paintings*

For paintings that are going to be taken carefully to storage, the easiest method is to get a mirror pack box from a moving company, put the painting inside, stuff some newspaper in the sides and tape it shut.

- ♦ Don't pack wet or humid artwork.
- ♦ Be sure to label the contents on the outside.

Another way is to buy sheets of cardboard and cut appropriate sizes (two or three layers is better that one!) to make a "painting sandwich." Bubble wrap can be added for further padding and protection.

- ♦ Don't skimp on the packing tape.
- ♦ Don't let the tape touch the frame.

Photographs and/or a video will be of great help when you have to file an insurance claim. It will also help to put back together badly broken items. Keep a copy at another location.

A fellow was storing a couple of paintings under his bed, cause he had no other place to put them (he said). Little did he know that his cat had chosen under the bed as its territory and play ground. A couple of nice paintings got badly thrashed.

Used by permission, Historic Mission Inn Corp.

Heat and humidity do bad things to paintings.

## *Supply Locator: Paintings*

| **Supply** | **Number or Other Resouce** |
|---|---|
| | (Numbers correspond to vendor number on next page.) |
| Baggies | 8, Supermarket |
| Brushes, artists', size 3-6 | 1, 3, 7, 8, Art store |
| Brushes, long bristles, painting | 1, 3, 8, Art store |
| Bubble wrap | Paper supply, Moving company |
| Cardboard | 8, Paper supply, Moving Co. |
| Cotton applicators | 1, 3, 8, Supermarket, Drug store |
| Dust Bunny | 1 |
| Fan | Home Improvement, Warehouse store |
| Foam, for packing | 7, check Yellow Pages under Foam Rubber and Sponge |
| Hammers | 1, 3, 8, Hardware store |
| Mirror box (cardboard) | Moving company |
| Paper towels | Supermarket |
| Plastic keys | Art store |
| Quake Wax | 1, 7, 8, Hardware stores |
| Rags | Paint store |
| Screws for concrete | 1, 3, 8, Hardware stores |
| Silicone release papers | 1, 2, 3, 8 |
| Skewer stick | 1, 3, 8, Supermarket |
| Soluvar | 1, 3, 8, Art store |
| Spatula, artist | 1, 3, 7, 8, Art store |
| Toilet paper | Supermarket |
| Toothpick | Supermarket |
| Wax paper | Supermarket |

# SUPPLIERS OF PRESERVATION MATERIALS

**When you cannot find what you need at the local store, here is a list of suppliers who will have the hard to find stuff. Call the #800 and ask for a free catalog. They are usually very informative. Also, the lists of materials mentioned from each chapter have numbers that match with the suppliers on this page, so you know who sells what.**

**1.** Conservation Materials Ltd.
Box 2884, Sparks, NV  89431
Phone Toll Free (800) 733-5283
Phone (702) 331-0582
Fax (702) 331-0588
General preservation supplies.  Has Collector Care Kits, scrapbooks and photo albums.

**2.** United Mfrs. Supplies, Inc.
80 Gordon Drive, Syosset, NY 11791
Phone Toll Free  (800) 645-7260
Fax:  (516) 496-7968
Hardware

**3.** Gaylord Archival Preservation & Conservation Supplies and Equipment
Box 4901, Syracuse, NY 13221
Phone Toll Free (800) 448-6160
Fax:  (800) 272-3412
General preservation supplies.

**4.** Vue-All Inc.
P.O. Box 1994, Ocala, FL  32678
Phone (904) 732-3188
Phone Toll Free (800) 874-9737
Fax:  (904) 867-8243
Specializes in good  quality photo sleeves and pages

**5.** Metal Edge West, Inc.
2721 East 45th St., L.A., CA 90058
Phone (213) 588-2228
Phone Toll Free (800) 862-2228
Fax: (213) 588-2150
Internet http://www.eden.com:8080/~midnight/avi/shoppe1.avi
General preservation supplies.

**6.** Light Impressions
439 Monroe Avenue, Rochester, NY   14607-3717
Phone  (716) 271-8960
Phone Toll Free  (800) 828-6216
Fax: (800) 828-5539
General preservation supplies, scrapbooks and photo albums.

**7.** University Products, Inc.
P.O. Box 101, Holyoke, MA   01041
Phone (413) 532-3372
Phone Toll Free (800) 628-1912
Fax (800) 532- 9281
General preservation supplies, scrapbooks and photo albums.

**8.** Conservation Support Systems
P.O. Box 91746 Santa Barbara, CA   93190
Phone (805) 682-9843
Phone Toll Free (800) 482-6299
Fax:  (805) 682-2064
General preservation supplies.

**9.** Bradley's Plastic Bag Co.
9130 Firestone Blvd. Downey, CA  90241
Phone (213) 923-5556
Phone (818) 289-0811
Phone Toll Free (800) 621-7864
Fax: (310) 862-4474
Plastic supplies of all kinds.

**10.** Archival Products
P.O. Box 1413, Des Moines, IA   50305
Phone Toll Free (800) 247-5323
Fax: (515) 262-6013
General preservation supplies.

**11.** Talas
213 W. 35th St., New York, NY  10001-1996
Phone  (212) 219-0770
Fax: (212) 219-0735
General preservation supplies.  Specializes in textile supplies.

**12.** Conservation Resources
800-H Forbes Place, Springfield, VA  22151
Phone Toll Free (800) 634-6932
Fax: (703) 321-0629
General preservation supplies.

# CHAPTER 8

## Framing

### *Before a disaster occurs:*

**How bad framing hurts**

Framing a certificate or artwork does not necessarily preserve or protect it. In fact, here are a few ways that framing jobs can be a real disaster:

1. Trimming the artwork (reduces the value).

2. Use of masking tape or scotch tape (causes yellowing stains, which continue to get darker with time, and will become impossible to remove).

3. Use of contact cement (causes yellow and brown stains, which continue to get darker with time, and will become impossible to remove).

4. Use of white glue (will yellow and be very difficult to remove).

5. Dry mounting (turns yellow brown, very difficult to free artwork/certificate later and absorbs into the paper a permanent waxy goop that will get more yellow with time and will not come out).

6. Cardboard backing board (turns good paper acidic and accelerates the yellowing, embrittlement and aging of all papers, causes bad acid stains).

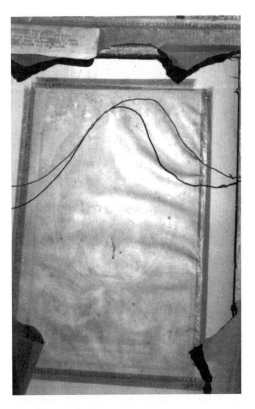

The frame job from hell: Trimmed art work, masking tape around the edge, acid matts, cardboard backing, thin hanging wire, tiny eye screws (about to fall out).

7. Mat boards which are not acid-free (turns good paper acidic and accelerated the yellowing, embrittlement and aging of all papers, causes bad acid stains).

Within very little time (a year?) these uglies can begin to noticeably deteriorate the framed item. This accelerates the aging process and reduces or eliminates any financial value your item may have. If you're out shopping for framed artwork, buyers beware.

**How does light harm framed items?**

It is also very important to remember that by hanging something on the wall, it doesn't take a lot of light to irretrievably do the following:

1. Day light will change or fade colors (especially watercolors, textiles, leathers and natural products).

2. Day light will change or fade hand written inks (especially ball point pen).

3. Day light will change, fade and embrittle silks and other fabrics, plastics.

4. Day light will hasten the yellowing/darkening of many low quality papers.

5. Fluorescent lights will change or fade colors in prints and textiles.

The damage does not happen, POW!, all in one day. It happens minute by minute, day by day, every day. If you have questions about your particular item, call a professional conservator that specializes in your item or call the local museum curator for advice. Art gallery owners usually don't have a clue, even the "best high quality galleries" in the big cities, though they will rarely admit it.

## *A Guide for Proper Framing*

When you have something framed make sure the materials (glues, tapes) the framer uses to attach the artwork (or item) in the mats or onto the backing board are "reversible." This means that the paper item can be removed from

Acids (the wrong pH) cause paper to change color (yellow or brown), become brittle, "grow" spots called "foxing" and, generally speaking, to deteriorate quickly.

Acid-free means that the acids have been neutralized or removed. But it doesn't mean the acids can't show up in the future. In fact, they probably will.

Buffered means that there is a time release cold capsule inside the paper that releases acid busters when they are needed. Therefore, the paper stays acid-free and safe.

the frame in its original condition (without damage) at any time in the future and the glue, adhesive or tape can be removed completely without hurting the paper. See my list of the ten most wanted uglies (to be shot on sight) at the beginning of the book.

## Your Item Being Framed:

Never trim the paper if you want to keep its value (financial or historic). Dry mounting will cause the paper to yellow and it will very difficult (an expensive) to get off later. In fact, don't glue a paper item down to any-thing... better to have a little waviness in the paper. Also, make sure the framed item does not touch the glass, especially if it's a pastel, chalk or crayon.

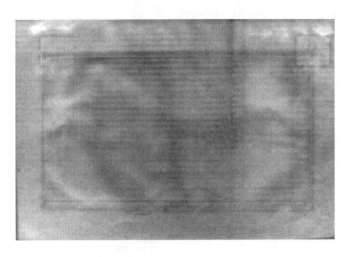

Cardboard acid stains on the <u>back</u> of the framed paper. Very common, Very bad...

## Window Mat:

Always use acid-free, buffered mat boards with a pH range of 7.5 to 8.5. If you can, make it 100% rag. Beware: some mat boards are advertised as acid-free but have only an acid-free outer paper! The inner core may be acidic and will cause damage. Don't accept "Museum board," "Ar-chival Board" or whatever unless you know it's buffered and acid-free through and through.  Use at least 4 ply for the mat (6 or 8 ply looks very nice). It provides the rec-ommended air space between the item being framed and the glass. There is really no reason to use an acidic board but if the framer talks you into it then, at least, a two ply acid-free buffered is necessary between the framed item and the mat board (barrier sheet). The framer may want to use  pieces of scrap for this but insist that it be a single piece of paper and have it extend to the opening of the window of the mat.  Much of the yellowing and stains from acid migration from acidic mat boards come from the groundwood core which is exposed when cut.

## Back Mat:

Completely acid-free buffered 4 ply board should be used. Don't use (gulp) cardboard!

Mr. Acid Free Buffered:
Nothing gets by him!

**Backing Board:**

ditto

**Hinges:**

The best method of attaching a paper item or photo into the mat is with two (or three if a large work) lightweight paper hinges. Conservators and quality framers often use a Japanese papers for the hinge and attach them with starch paste. Make sure the hinges are placed only at the top of the item and not all around the sides and bottom of the paper (which will cause warping and wavyness). This allows the paper to expand or contract without cockling. Remember, the glue (or paste) used for hinging must be reversible (like starch paste or methyl cellulose or ethulose). Do not use any kind of pressure sensitive tape, rubber cement, glue, etc. if you have preservation in mind. Some acid-free, reversible, conservation tapes may be OK for this work but most of them will give away and let go of the artwork after awhile. Consult with a paper conservator, high quality framer or museum preparator.

Glass (or Plexiglas like materials can be used) but these materials do not filter out UV light which causes fading. You can buy a UV filtering Plexiglas (UF3 or UF4) which will reduce but will not eliminate the possibility of fading. Also, with Plexiglas some items like pastels, charcoals and other powdery materials must be held away from the art work at least 3/8" or 1/2" because of an electrostatic charge.

**Framing molding:**

Don't let paper items come in direct contact with the wood. It is very acidic and will quickly cause the paper to yellow, stain, embrittle etc.

**Dust Cover:**

Use a dust cover on the back of all frames to protect against dust and insects. It is not required to use acid-free buffered materials (because they are not in contact with the artwork/framed item) but they will last longer and look better over the years.

**These are a few other very important reminders:**

♦ Make sure the screw eyes and wire are in good shape (not frayed or loose). You can buy replacement materials from your local art store or see "Suppliers."

♦ Make sure the hanging hook is well anchored. In an earthquake a loose fitting hook will give away. When putting up an hanging hook, try to hit and anchor the hook into a stud. If this is not possible, or if you are trying to hang something on a cement wall buy the right kind of expanding sleeves for the screw (to be used in place of the nail) from the hardware store.

♦ Use a couple of balls of Quake Wax between the wall and the frame to hold the frame where you put it (so it doesn't keep going skeewampus) and it will also hold more securely in an earthquake. See "Where to buy" at end of book.

Photographs of individual valuable items and/or a video will be of great help when you have to file an insurance claim. It will also help to put back together badly broken items. Keep a copy at another location.

*After the Northridge Earthquake in L.A., I had a variety of items come in that had been cut by broken glass: paintings, vintage movies posters, Hollywood memorabilia, wedding certificates, engravings.*

## *After a disaster occurs:*

### If an earthquake occurs:

Be careful of broken glass (a good reason to use Plexiglas) not only for your feet but be careful not to let the broken glass scratch the framed item. Handle with extreme care even if you think you have removed all

*Put broken pieces in a zip lock bag, label, staple to back of frame. Look to see if other pieces are about to fall off.*

the pieces of glass. There are always little slivers and chips around that can still do a lot of damage. Take the item to your framer. If you paid attention to the advice in the previous section, you will be very happy that the glues used to mount in the framed item were reversible.

If you are like most people, the items you have framed may be some of the most important items you own. Therefore, in the aftermath of damage, first take care of carefully and thoughtfully saving and protecting these items. You may be sifting through a lot of dirty objects so wear gloves and don't get the framed items more dirty from your hands. It is possible to cause more damage in the clean up effort that occurred from the disaster.

Frames are fragile items that often get knocked around and damaged. If an ornate frame or antique frame has been broken, all the loose pieces should be gathered, kept in a zip-lock bag and then stapled to the back of the frame. To get your frame repaired, you can:

1. Contact a framer, (who will usually do the worst quality-cheapest job) or

2. Contact a frame conservator. Find someone who does good quality gold (vs. metal) leafing. He / she will usually have the skills to do the best job even if you don't need gilding or

3. You can give it a shot yourself.

**Here is how to try a frame repair at home:**

1. Give yourself room to work, unencumbered by other repair projects, tools and mess.

2. It's easier to work with the frame lying face down. Put pads under corners, especially if they are ornate, so they don't get knocked off. Rags, rolls of paper, a tube of carpet taped closed, foam pads will do.

3. Remove and throw away all screws, nails, wire. Take them from the frame and put them directly into the trash. You should put on new hardware when you are done. See "Where to Buy."

4. Clean off surface, easy to remove, dust, dirt, etc. Wipe quickly with soft, slightly damp, cloth. This could damage some frame finishes so do a small test in a non noticeable area. If you're not sure, call a frame conservator.

5. The frame's surface should not be damp or wet but if it is, wipe quickly with a dry rag.

6. Give the surface a finish coat with a clear carnauba wax, gently applied with cotton tipped applicators and buffed off. This will also help clean the surface of the frame. This could damage some frame finishes so do a small test in a non noticeable area. If you're not sure, call a frame conservator.

7. Detached pieces of frames can be reglued into their original position with white glue (see "where to buy" for conservation quality glues). Use small clamps or rubber bands (test cautiously) to hold the pieces in place. Woodworking clamps can be bought at hobby stores. Reglue loose (but not detached) pieces through cracks in surface with white glue (diluted 30%). Plastic syringes can be bought in hobby stores for getting the glue into small places.

8. Missing areas can be filled in by "painting with plaster", thick plaster of Paris mixture painted with brush. Make small amounts in disposable container, make only as much as you can use in 20 minutes (warmer water sets plaster quicker). Rinse brush in bowl of water before rinsing under faucet. DO NOT throw leftover plaster mixture down drain because it will clog it. Wait to harden and throw away.

Courtesy Conservation Materials, Ltd.

A conservation quality glue.

9. Cracks and losses can sometimes be adequately camouflaged with watercolors. Tone to match gold frames with "gold dust" (see "Where to Buy") mixed into varnish and/ or watercolor.

### *Fire Damage*

**If there has been a fire: There will be soot, smoke, dirt and possibly water damage (see next paragraph on flooding).**

♦ Protect the frame against more dirt and soot.

♦ Wipe the frame down to get off loose dirt and soot. See instructions above for cleaning.

♦ See instructions above for removing the item from the framing or...

♦ Take everything to a good framer who will carefully take things a part for you.

Once the items have been separated from their frames and are apart, you can decide what you want reframed.

### *Water Damage*

**If water damage has occurred you need to get the frame dried out, period. DO:**

♦ Use fans to get the room temperature air circulating.

♦ Rent a dehumidifier?

♦ Air-conditioned air will help to dry things out.

♦ Be extremely careful when handling.

**DON'T:**

♦ Don't put things in the sun to dry. Plaster layers will crack and warp out of shape. Ornaments will crack and peel off.

♦ Don't use a blow dryer and get the frame hot for the same reasons as above.

While this condition may be alarming, you will be glad to know that upon allowing the frame to dry completely, it will re-harden and may not need special care or treatments later.

♦ Don't turn on the heaters unless you want to grow
   a crop of mold.

If you cannot get it out of the wet, humid situation within
48 hours (mold will begin to grow), you could freeze it.
Check with commercial meat handlers, ice cream mak-
ers, restaurants or something similar to see who has a
freezer big enough.

**To prepare a frame for freezing:**

♦ Handle it as little as possible because it will fall
   apart especially if it has plaster on it.

♦ Wrap it in plastic.

♦ Don't put pressure on any wet areas.

♦ Handle it like it was very thin broken glass.

Be especially careful when handling wet frames and
framed items: everything falls apart easily.  If possible,
remove the mat boards and the framed item together from
the frame and glass. Use extreme caution if you try and
separate the mat boards or remove the artwork while they
are wet (See "Art on Paper").

If your frame is wet and if it is made out of plaster or has
plaster type decorations, then handling the frame will be
very precarious.  When wet, gesso becomes soft and the
details of the frame may pulverize in your hands.  Let the
frame dry out by circulating the air with a fan.
Do not put the wet frame in the sun and do not use a blow
dryer as you may cause plaster, compo ornamentation,
wood carving or finishes to crack.

## *Handling and Storage*

Be aware that if you have taken your frames off the wall,
that there are hooks, nails, wires, etc., on the back of the
frame which may badly scratch or otherwise damage furniture, paintings and other framed items onto which these
frames are leaned.

Something else to consider is the increasing value of old frames on the art market. Take good care of them, they may be worth more than you think.

**When wrapping a frame:**

Another option is to wrap with paper, wrap with plastic, tape closed, place in a mirror box and fill with "popcorn" styrofoam on all sides, top and bottom.

♦ Tissue paper or unprinted newsprint will keep wrapping materials from sticking to some finishes.

♦ Plastic bubble wrap will help to protect the corners and edges from chipping. Don't be skimpy on this stuff.

♦ You can cut two pieces of cardboard the size of the frame (or a little bigger) and putting one on front and one on the back, tape the whole sandwich together.

♦ Be careful not to let the tape touch the finish of the frame (very important).

♦ Or a "mirror box" can be purchased from a moving company for easy storage protection.

♦ Be sure to label the outside of the package (include a polaroid shot of the contents?) or you may not remember what's inside in six months (or if you are like me it'll only take you till tomorrow to forget).

## *Supply Locator: Paintings*

| **Supply** | **Number or Other Resource** |
| --- | --- |
| | (Numbers correspond to vendor number on next page.) |
| Bubble wrap, plastic | Paper Supply store, Moving Co. |
| Carnuba wax | 1, 3, 8 |
| Clamps, woodworking | 2, 3, 8, Hardware store |
| Cotton tipped applicators | 1, 3, 8, Supermarket, Drug store |
| Dehumidifier | 6, Home Improvement |
| Fans | Hardware store, Warehouse store |
| Gloves, white cotton | 1, 2, 3, 6, 7, 8, 12 |
| Hanging hooks | 2, 3, 6, 7, 8, Hardware store |
| Hinges, paper | 2, 3, 6, 7, 8 |
| Mats, acid-free buffered | 2, 3, 5, 6, 8, Art store |
| Methyl cellulose and ethulose | 1, 2, 3, 6, 7, 8, 12 |
| Pads, foam | 7, Look in Yellow Pages under Foam Rubber & Sponge |
| Plaster of Paris | 8 |
| Plexiglas, UF3 and UF4 | 2, 3, 6, 8, 12, Glass store, Frame shop |
| Quake Wax | 1, 7, 8, Hardware store, Museum shop |
| Rags | Paint store |
| Screw eyes | 1, 2, 3, 6, 8, Hardware store |
| Screws for concrete | 1, 2, 3, 8, Hardware store |
| Starch paste | 1, 2, 3, 6, 7, 8, 12 |
| Syringes | 1, 3, 8, Hobby store |
| Tapes, conservation | 1, 2, 3, 6, 7, 8, 12 |
| Tissue paper | 1, 3, 6, 7, 8, 12, Art store, Drug store |
| White glue | 1, 2, 3, 6, 7, 8, 12 |
| Wire, hanging, plastic coated | 2, 3, Hardware store |

# SUPPLIERS OF PRESERVATION MATERIALS

**When you cannot find what you need at the local store, here is a list of suppliers who will have the hard to find stuff. Call the #800 and ask for a free catalog. They are usually very informative. Also, the lists of materials mentioned from each chapter have numbers that match with the suppliers on this page, so you know who sells what.**

**1.** Conservation Materials Ltd.
Box 2884, Sparks, NV 89431
Phone Toll Free (800) 733-5283
Phone (702) 331-0582
Fax (702) 331-0588
General preservation supplies. Has Collector Care Kits, scrapbooks and photo albums.

**2.** United Mfrs. Supplies, Inc.
80 Gordon Drive, Syosset, NY 11791
Phone Toll Free (800) 645-7260
Fax: (516) 496-7968
Hardware

**3.** Gaylord Archival Preservation & Conservation Supplies and Equipment
Box 4901, Syracuse, NY 13221
Phone Toll Free (800) 448-6160
Fax: (800) 272-3412
General preservation supplies.

**4.** Vue-All Inc.
P.O. Box 1994, Ocala, FL 32678
Phone (904) 732-3188
Phone Toll Free (800) 874-9737
Fax: (904) 867-8243
Specializes in good quality photo sleeves and pages

**5.** Metal Edge West, Inc.
2721 East 45th St., L.A., CA 90058
Phone (213) 588-2228
Phone Toll Free (800) 862-2228
Fax: (213) 588-2150
Internet http://www.eden.com:8080/~midnight/avi/shoppe1.avi
General preservation supplies.

**6.** Light Impressions
439 Monroe Avenue, Rochester, NY 14607-3717
Phone (716) 271-8960
Phone Toll Free (800) 828-6216
Fax: (800) 828-5539
General preservation supplies, scrapbooks and photo albums.

**7.** University Products, Inc.
P.O. Box 101, Holyoke, MA 01041
Phone (413) 532-3372
Phone Toll Free (800) 628-1912
Fax (800) 532- 9281
General preservation supplies, scrapbooks and photo albums.

**8.** Conservation Support Systems
P.O. Box 91746 Santa Barbara, CA 93190
Phone (805) 682-9843
Phone Toll Free (800) 482-6299
Fax: (805) 682-2064
General preservation supplies.

**9.** Bradley's Plastic Bag Co.
9130 Firestone Blvd. Downey, CA 90241
Phone (213) 923-5556
Phone (818) 289-0811
Phone Toll Free (800) 621-7864
Fax: (310) 862-4474
Plastic supplies of all kinds.

**10.** Archival Products
P.O. Box 1413, Des Moines, IA 50305
Phone Toll Free (800) 247-5323
Fax: (515) 262-6013
General preservation supplies.

**11.** Talas
213 W. 35th St., New York, NY 10001-1996
Phone (212) 219-0770
Fax: (212) 219-0735
General preservation supplies. Specializes in textile supplies.

**12.** Conservation Resources
800-H Forbes Place, Springfield, VA 22151
Phone Toll Free (800) 634-6932
Fax: (703) 321-0629
General preservation supplies.

# CHAPTER 9

# Rugs, Tapestries and Old Clothes

## *Before a disaster occurs:*

There is a big difference between old cloth items and ones made recently: vintage cloth items (handmade?) have been weakened by use, cleaning, light, bugs and the natural aging of the materials. Recently made items (machine made?) contain synthetics and should be stronger. They usually have not been exposed to the above named problems. Take note as you handle, try on, fold, store, etc. your textiles.

**Your heirlooms are special!**

- ◆ Don't yank a, rug let's say, from under a pile of things, as the stress may pull the item apart and break threads. Remove things sitting on top of an heirloom first.

- ◆ Resist the temptation to wear or walk on heirlooms.

- ◆ Use them for display on a guest bed or as a wall hanging (but be sure its supported correctly and don't let it get much light!).

♦ Limit the sunlight (direct or indirect) or fluorescent light.

♦ Declaw your cat before it picks your heirloom apart.

♦ Don't use liquids to spot clean.

♦ Don't locate heirlooms where spills can occur.

♦ Consult a textile conservator before attempting to deep clean an heirloom. You could even ask for suggestions on how to hang it up on the wall (before you use the technique of pounding nails through it).

On the left, a six inch tube (this size or larger is good). On the right, a 1 1/2 inch tube (too small)!

To protect and preserve tapestries and rugs during storage, wrap them around a wide, sturdy tube:
(Try not to fold old big heavy textiles, especially older rugs and tapestries where creases may deform or even weaken the fabric.)

1. Prior to rolling the textile on a tube, the tube should be wrapped with clean paper (butcher paper is OK), plastic (visqueen) or a clean white cotton sheet.

2. Before you roll it up be sure that the fabric is dry.

3. Roll the textile around a tube that is longer than the item. Cardboard tubes can be obtained from carpet stores or construction material supply houses (Sono tubes). A diameter of 4"-8" (small items) 6"-10" (large or stiff items) is recommended depending on the size of the rug. Only one textile should be stored on each tube because layering rugs and tapestries may cause them to slide to one end of the roll and get crumpled when the tube gets stood on end.

Rugs ready for storage: Rolled around a tube with a silverfish tab inside, wrapped with butcher paper, taped closed and labeled.

4. Do not wrap the textile around a small tube (4" or less) too tightly. It will cause wrinkles, dimples and waviness that will set in the fabric.

5. Also you may want to put a moth ball on the inside of the tube for discouraging any pests (put a couple in an old sock and staple it to the inside of the tube so it does not come in contact with the fabric).

6. A sheet of butcher paper may be wrapped around the outside of the textile for protection. If you are tempted to wrap the whole thing in plastic, consider that if you live in a humid area, that you will probably grow mold. On the other hand, plastic keeps out bugs and varmints.

7. You can tie the whole thing closed with strips of fabric.

8. Before you put your textile into storage, label it on the outside of the packaging. Do not use indelible (permanent) inks that would soak through the sheet and permanently stain the textile. Paper stickum labels or tape will not adhere for very long (especially on the plastic); a tag with a string works well.

**For heirloom clothing, make sure the item is well supported as you carry it around:**

♦ Use a well padded hanger if the fabric is strong enough to support it's own weight.

♦ Use a slip cover.

♦ Use acid-free buffered storage boxes or proper plastic containers (Tupperware or Rubbermaid), acid-free tissue wrapping paper and padding (to avoid hard folds) when placing items in flat storage.

♦ Use packets of moth balls in closed storage. Remember, don't let the moth balls touch the fabric. This will not guarantee the elimination of pests. However, they don't like this stuff so maybe they will go to the other side of the closet and eat your husband's camel overcoat instead. You can put the moth balls in a clean old sock.

*RRRIP!*

Photographs of individual valuable items and/or a video will be of great help when you have to file an insurance claim. It will also help to put back together badly broken items. Keep a copy at another location.

## *After a disaster occurs:*

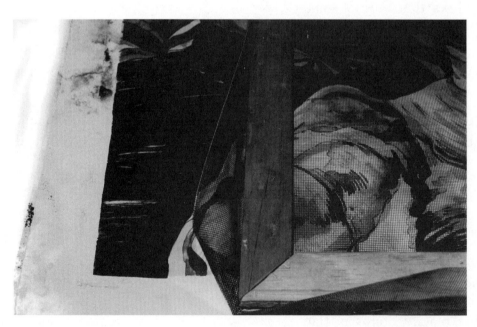

The dirt on this needle point can be vacuumed up through the screen without damaging the yarns with the metal nozzle-especially important if it is old.

Rugs, tapestries and vintage clothes are usually not damaged in an earthquake unless exposed to water. If there is a bunch of stuff on top of your textile, don't yank, the rug let's say, free from under the pile, as the stress may pull the item apart and break threads. Remove things sitting on top of the heirloom first. Be sure to wear a mask! The dust from the building materials is often toxic and is everywhere after an earthquake.

## *Vacuuming:*

Not only for general care but in a disaster you may need to remove dust and debris or use a wet/dry vacuum to remove water. Do not vacuum directly on old materials, especially if wet. When the fabric gets caught in the suction, it will damage the material.

Vacuum your textile through a piece of plastic window screen (available for under $1 per yard from your local hardware shop) and you will reduce the risk of sucking up your heirloom.

◆ It's as easy as laying a piece of regular window screening on the fabric and vacuuming, but a heavy gauge (thick threads) screen with an open weave works best.

◆ I suggest you buy a plastic screen material, not metal which can rust and leave impurities in the fabric.

◆ Even better, get a set of stretcher bars from your local art store (no canvas, cost will be about $5.00) and with a stapler, stretch the screen over the wood frame for easy handling.

◆ The screen can be washed when dirty. Make sure your screen stays clean so you do not transfer dirt from one item to another.

## *Water Damage*

In case of water damage, which may also happen if a fire breaks out, be extra careful about handling these fragile items. Do not roll the wet rug up and stand it in a corner!

◆ Mold will grow.

◆ The weight of the rug will cause it to crumple and sag in on itself...

Wet items need to be dried out with 48 hours to minimize the mold problem.

♦ ... causing distortions and damage.

♦ The water will probably cause the colors to run.

If possible, keep rugs and tapestries prone, open and with fans moving room temperature air to dry them out.

Big flat items will be very difficult and fragile to move when wet; get some extra support underneath with some boards or plywood. But don't leave the wet items in contact with the wood! The water will dissolve impurities from the wood and the textile will be stained.

### Drying a textile

♦ Excess water can be blotted with clean rags and paper.

♦ Or try putting dry clean rags and paper on the item then rolling it up; then unroll, exchange wet rags for dry ones and reroll etc.

♦ When handling vintage clothing, be careful of buttons, beading, metal fasteners etc. as the wet fabric could easily rip away.

♦ Don't rub on the fabric as this will bring up a nap and damage the item.

♦ Wet items need to be dried out with 48 hours to minimize the mold problem (and rust/corrosion if there are metal pieces attached).

♦ Never place rugs and tapestries in the sun to dry. Most textiles, especially old ones, are decorated with colors that fade and if placed in the sun extensive fading and color change could result quickly.

If getting things dried out safely is not possible, small items can be placed in the freezer to buy some extra time.

♦ Separate several items with sheets of wax paper to keep them from sticking together and to keep the colors from running off one item to the next.

After the death of a sweet grandmother, it was discovered that she had preserved important newspaper clippings, personal letters and poetry between the hand embroidered linens (that she had done) in her linen drawers. The acids from the newspaper clippings had caused extensive staining and yellowing on everything that they touched and more: some of the poetry pages were so bad they could hardly be read and the ugly stains sadly marred many of the beautiful linens.

Check the bottles of soap at the store to see if they say "non-ionic." If they don't... they aren't... so don't use them.

A product I like is a detergent called "Orvus." It comes in a paste. It can be bought from Conservation Materials Ltd. I've heard that it is also repackaged and used in the sheep industry for washing the fuzzy animals so you may find the soap at your local livestock supply store. Try it on your dog!

- ♦ Wrap in plastic and seal.
- ♦ Never store wet textiles.
- ♦ Never wash or work on more than one item at a time.

Freeze drying may be the best way to get several large items dry if you don't have room. Call local commercial drying facilities.

For stain removal, you may test a stained area by blotting (don't rub!) the color to see if they are stable. Then test again using a non ionic soap. If, in fact, the colors are stable then use white paper towels below and above the item and blot (don't rub!) the stained area. Change the paper towels often. Remember, the spot and the fabric are darker when wet. After everything is dry the colors will be much lighter. All areas so treated should be thoroughly rinsed (did I mention that you should blot not rub?) with distilled water and dried in a ventilated area. Fresh stains can be harder to get out at a later date. If you try to dry a wet spot with a blow dryer, the stain may set and be more difficult to remove later. On the other hand, nothing should remain wet for more than 48 hours (mold).

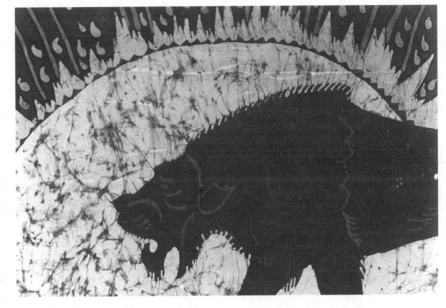

This silk textile was stored folded. It broke and fell apart at the fold.

A good drying rack might be the collapsible nylon netting on a frame that is sold for drying sweaters in the bathroom. But don't use a flimsy frame for a heavy rug. Call a professional textile conservator no matter what you do. He/she can help you to decide if a commercial cleaner will be OK, if you should attempt a stain removal yourself, or if he/she needs to see the damaged item. A quick consultation session for a single item/problem with a private professional is often free and will be very helpful.

## *Supply Locator: Rugs, Tapestries & Old Clothes*

**Supply**                                      **Number or Other Resource**

(Numbers correspond to vendor number on next page.)

Boxes, acid free buffered storage ................................. 3, 5, 6, 7, 8, 10, 12
Butcher paper .............................................................. Paper Supply store
Containers, plastic (Tupperware or Rubbermaid) .......... Supermarket, Drug store, Warehouse store
Garment bag ............................................................... Department store
Hangers, padded ......................................................... 3, 8, Department store
Mask, dust .................................................................. 3, 7, 8, Hardware store
Moth balls .................................................................. Hardware store, Home Improvement store
Non-ionic soap ........................................................... 3, Supermarket
Orvus ......................................................................... 1, 7, 8
Plastic tarp ................................................................. Hardware store, Home Improvement store
Rags ........................................................................... Paint store
Screening, window ...................................................... Hardware store, Home Improvement store
Tags, string ................................................................ 3, 5, 7, Office Supply store
Tissue paper, acid free ................................................ 3, 6, 7, 8, 12
Tubes, cardboard ........................................................ 3, 7, 8, Carpet store
Visqueen .................................................................... Hardware store, Home Improvement store
Water, distilled ........................................................... Supermarket
Wax paper .................................................................. Supermarket

# SUPPLIERS OF PRESERVATION MATERIALS

**When you cannot find what you need at the local store, here is a list of suppliers who will have the hard to find stuff. Call the #800 and ask for a free catalog. They are usually very informative. Also, the lists of materials mentioned from each chapter have numbers that match with the suppliers on this page, so you know who sells what.**

**1.** Conservation Materials Ltd.
Box 2884, Sparks, NV 89431
Phone Toll Free (800) 733-5283
Phone (702) 331-0582
Fax (702) 331-0588
General preservation supplies. Has Collector Care Kits, scrapbooks and photo albums.

**2.** United Mfrs. Supplies, Inc.
80 Gordon Drive, Syosset, NY 11791
Phone Toll Free (800) 645-7260
Fax: (516) 496-7968
Hardware

**3.** Gaylord Archival Preservation & Conservation Supplies and Equipment
Box 4901, Syracuse, NY 13221
Phone Toll Free (800) 448-6160
Fax: (800) 272-3412
General preservation supplies.

**4.** Vue-All Inc.
P.O. Box 1994, Ocala, FL 32678
Phone (904) 732-3188
Phone Toll Free (800) 874-9737
Fax: (904) 867-8243
Specializes in good quality photo sleeves and pages

**5.** Metal Edge West, Inc.
2721 East 45th St., L.A., CA 90058
Phone (213) 588-2228
Phone Toll Free (800) 862-2228
Fax: (213) 588-2150
Internet http://www.eden.com:8080/~midnight/avi/shoppe1.avi
General preservation supplies.

**6.** Light Impressions
439 Monroe Avenue, Rochester, NY 14607-3717
Phone (716) 271-8960
Phone Toll Free (800) 828-6216
Fax: (800) 828-5539
General preservation supplies, scrapbooks and photo albums.

**7.** University Products, Inc.
P.O. Box 101, Holyoke, MA 01041
Phone (413) 532-3372
Phone Toll Free (800) 628-1912
Fax (800) 532- 9281
General preservation supplies, scrapbooks and photo albums.

**8.** Conservation Support Systems
P.O. Box 91746 Santa Barbara, CA 93190
Phone (805) 682-9843
Phone Toll Free (800) 482-6299
Fax: (805) 682-2064
General preservation supplies.

**9.** Bradley's Plastic Bag Co.
9130 Firestone Blvd. Downey, CA 90241
Phone (213) 923-5556
Phone (818) 289-0811
Phone Toll Free (800) 621-7864
Fax: (310) 862-4474
Plastic supplies of all kinds.

**10.** Archival Products
P.O. Box 1413, Des Moines, IA 50305
Phone Toll Free (800) 247-5323
Fax: (515) 262-6013
General preservation supplies.

**11.** Talas
213 W. 35th St., New York, NY 10001-1996
Phone (212) 219-0770
Fax: (212) 219-0735
General preservation supplies. Specializes in textile supplies.

**12.** Conservation Resources
800-H Forbes Place, Springfield, VA 22151
Phone Toll Free (800) 634-6932
Fax: (703) 321-0629
General preservation supplies.

# CHAPTER 10

# Sculpture and Furniture

## *Before a disaster occurs:*

Sculpture, like furniture, comes in many shapes, sizes and materials so it is difficult to tell you exactly what to do (without actually seeing your item). Generally speaking, the following steps can be taken to protect your objects against disasters:

♦ Small to medium sized objects can be anchored down with Quake Wax, a sticky synthetic wax that can be used between the base of the object and the table top or shelf. The object can be picked up at any time and Quake Wax will not stain the furniture surface. Other materials like Plastellina or other "fixing" or anchoring materials can contain oils or materials that should be avoided as they can stain furniture and objects alike.

Whether it's earthquakes or grandkids, he's there to help.

If some of these suggestions sound like they may challenge your handyman skills, call around to see if there is someone who can earthquake proof your house. I know of companies that specialize in this service in Los Angeles and San Francisco. Also, I have heard of cleaning ladies who have added earthquake proofing to their services. You could also call a "disaster relief" or "emergency response" company for a referral.

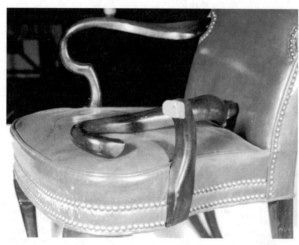

♦ Big heavy objects can be lassoed with fishing line in an inconspicuous place and tied to a eye screw in the wall or onto the furniture (don't sink a screw into your good furniture...). Anchor it from a couple of different directions so it won't "walk away" when the shaking starts.

♦ Large empty items like ceramics will be stabilized by a good sized bean bag or weight placed inside (diving weights?).

♦ Install clasps or hooks on cabinet doors.

♦ During a good shaker, tall or top heavy furniture will topple over. Behind the furniture, install anchor bolts (long eye screws) into the studs (not just into the plaster) and tie the furniture to the wall with a nylon coated wire. This type of wire can be bought in the form of picture hanging wire in heavy gauge. Nylon coated wire won't rust and the picture hanging wire is specially treated to be extra strong in relation to it's thickness or gauge. See "Where to Buy" at end of book.

♦ Replace glass shelves in cabinets (which will break and crash down on other items... they are heavy too) with Lucite or Plexiglas shelves. They can be made to order at your local glass shop. You can make sure the shelf stays put by putting a ball of Quake Wax between the shelf and the shelf brace.

A situation when objects often get broken is during a move from one location to another. I cannot emphasize enough the value of adding some bubble wrap and cardboard to the usual newspaper packing method. Materials may be bought from moving companies (like U-Haul) or party and paper supply companies. Or ask for a referral from a builder's supply company. Bulk purchases are a lot cheaper than a small roll from your local home improvement center.

Photographs of individual valuable items and/or a video will be of great help when you have to file an insurance claim. It will also help to put back together badly broken items. Keep a copy at another location.

## *After a disaster has occurred:*

**Earthquakes:**

**If there are broken pieces of sculpture and furniture:**

♦ Pieces should be kept together in a baggie or cardboard box.

♦ If the pieces are large enough, you may wrap each individual piece in a tissue paper (paper towel, tissue, etc.) so that the individual pieces do not knock around into each other.

♦ Protect pieces and items from getting dirty.

Do not attempt to move large pieces of broken furniture. Your back may not like it and you will probably further damage the furniture. Large furniture and sculpture are often made of many pieces glued together. These joints may be the first to give away.

Check broken furniture carefully before using them for working surfaces or for storage during clean-up after the earthquake. The additional weight may be the straw that breaks the camel's back (and all the items worth saving will end up on the floor, more broken than before).

It would be dangerous for me to suggest a glue to be used for gluing back to-gether broken sculpture and furniture, in general. The

During a move, unbeknownst to a dear friend, a prized arm chair was broken. In the new house, the chair went into her son's room where, shortly thereafter, the split in the wood gave way, causing bad splintering and breakage of the wood. Fortunately, her son wasn't hurt but the restoration bill is going to be much higher now.

Don't use epoxy on anything!

types of glues and other materials to reattach loose pieces depend on what material the object is made of. Contact a conservator for more specific suggestions.

A general warning is in order: If you try to repair your broken item yourself with a "permanent" (non reversible) adhesive, three things are likely to happen:

1. Even within a short time, the adhesive is likely to yellow, becoming unsightly.

2. Then, because it is "permanent", it will be very difficult (and expensive) to undo without further damaging the artwork. In other words, you may have succeeded in reattaching a broken piece, but in the end, you may cause more damage than was created by the disaster.

3. Many glues become hard and brittle to the point of breaking off additional pieces of the original object.

In the chaos of recuperating from a disaster, it is not a good idea to just start randomly gluing things together. Step back, take a breath. Get settled and plan calmly. Most objects/sculpture in stone, ceramic and glass are not going to get any worse once they are broken, if you take care while handling. So, you have time to plan what to do. Contact a conservator for more specific suggestions.

**In the event of water damage:**

♦ Get room temperature air moving (fans) around the objects immediately.

♦ Lower the humidity (rent a dehumidifier and turn on the air conditioning).

♦ Do not turn on the heat or you will accelerate the growth of mold.

**The following suggestions may offer some help in the event of a flood:**

♦ Remove mud and debris with clean water, drain and blot excess water (be very careful of painted surfaces or sculpture that is made from multiple pieces of materials). Blot, blot, blot and wear gloves. Be careful. Mud can be very abrasive when rubbed over a surface.

♦ Remove wet contents from drawers, blot the water out of the drawers, then replace the drawers into the furniture.

*If they are dried separately, the wood may distort and they may not go back together after drying.*

♦ If the item is made from wood, don't add heat so as to dry out the wood too quickly and cause cracking. The object should probably be loosely draped in plastic sheeting (visqueen) and the fans should not be blowing directly on the object. Drying should take place over a 72 hour period. Afterwards, the item should be wrapped in plastic for another 48 hours to let the humidity content inside the wood equalize. Then all that is left to do is hope it doesn't crack. If it is old wood (worm-eaten or previously damaged), it will be very fragile.

*Visqueen is used by contractors to cover roofs if its going to rain and by insulation contractors. It comes in a roll up to 16' wide and 100's of yards long. You can buy it in black, white and clear.*

♦ If mold develops on undecorated surfaces, wipe off the surface with a 50/50% mixture of water and denatured or isopropyl alcohol (buy from your drug store). Wipe the surface dry with a soft cloth.

*Keep items wrapped in plastic and out of the sunny warm areas or they will grow mold in an afternoon.*

♦ Expect varnished or lacquered surfaces to turn white or cloudy. This does not hurt the furniture. Consult with a conservator to reverse the problem.

*If you do see paint coming off, don't try to fix it.*

If the object is painted or decorated, be careful in handling, movement, etc.

The surface of the sculpture under the paint probably has glues that soften with water. The paint will come off in your hand easily. Be aware that if the object has been standing in water, that it is probable that once dry, the

*Let the weights sit for a few days.*

paint will begin to peel off. Therefore, the item should be stored in an area where it will not be moved, bumped, or brushed up against or handled and a professional conservator should be called immediately.

♦ If joints are weak on wooden furniture, they can be reinforced and bound up with strips of slit bicycle tubes, sheeting or other cloth. Then handle with care and do not drag or stack!

♦ Furniture with lifting veneer should be dried under weights to hold veneer in place. Put a piece of wax paper between the weight and the table top. It is probable that the glue will hold again when dry.

♦ Upholstered furniture: Spray off mud, blot wood dry, remove cushions, wrap in clean sheeting to wick out water. Keep the room temperature air moving! Handle with gloves. Call a professional cleaning company or a conservator if they are historic or of value.

If you put a little liquid carnuba wax(not paste-it leaves white deposits) on the end of the cotton tipped appliator it will clean better. Be sure to change the cotton swab when dirty.

♦ Metal objects, generally speaking, if wet, should be air dried off as soon as possible. This is especially true for items that will rust or where paint will be affected. It is generally a good idea to keep objects out of direct sunlight and out of cold water, as many adhesives used in some sculpture will be deteriorated by harsh elements. Therefore, it is best to keep them sheltered.

# *Supply Locator: Furniture and Sculpture*

| **Supply** | **Number or Other Resource** |
|---|---|
| | (Numbers correspond to vendor number on next page.) |
| Alcohol, denatured | 1, 8, Paint store, Drug store |
| Alcohol, isopropyl | 1, 8, Supermarket, Drug store |
| Baggies | 8, Supermarket |
| Bags, bean | 1, 8 |
| Bicycle tubes | Bicycle store |
| Bubble wrap | Paper Supply store, Moving company |
| Cardboard | 8, Paper store, Moving company |
| Dehumidifier | Home Improvement store, Warehouse store |
| Fan, electric | Home Improvement store, Warehouse store |
| Gloves, latex | 1, 3, 7, 8, Surgical Supply store |
| Gloves, white cotton | 1, 2, 3, 7, 8, 12 |
| Quake Wax | 1, 7, 8 |
| Screws, eye | 1, 2, 3, 8, Hardware store |
| Tissue paper | 1, 7, 8, Stationary store |
| Towels, paper | Supermarket |
| Visqueen | Building Supply store, Home Improvement store |
| Weights, diving | 8, Diving shop, Sports Supply store |

# SUPPLIERS OF PRESERVATION MATERIALS

**When you cannot find what you need at the local store, here is a list of suppliers who will have the hard to find stuff. Call the #800 and ask for a free catalog. They are usually very informative. Also, the lists of materials mentioned from each chapter have numbers that match with the suppliers on this page, so you know who sells what.**

**1.** Conservation Materials Ltd.
Box 2884, Sparks, NV 89431
Phone Toll Free (800) 733-5283
Phone (702) 331-0582
Fax (702) 331-0588
General preservation supplies. Has Collector Care Kits, scrapbooks and photo albums.

**2.** United Mfrs. Supplies, Inc.
80 Gordon Drive, Syosset, NY 11791
Phone Toll Free (800) 645-7260
Fax: (516) 496-7968
Hardware

**3.** Gaylord Archival Preservation & Conservation Supplies and Equipment
Box 4901, Syracuse, NY 13221
Phone Toll Free (800) 448-6160
Fax: (800) 272-3412
General preservation supplies.

**4.** Vue-All Inc.
P.O. Box 1994, Ocala, FL 32678
Phone (904) 732-3188
Phone Toll Free (800) 874-9737
Fax: (904) 867-8243
Specializes in good quality photo sleeves and pages

**5.** Metal Edge West, Inc.
2721 East 45th St., L.A., CA 90058
Phone (213) 588-2228
Phone Toll Free (800) 862-2228
Fax: (213) 588-2150
Internet http://www.eden.com:8080/~midnight/avi/shoppe1.avi
General preservation supplies.

**6.** Light Impressions
439 Monroe Avenue, Rochester, NY 14607-3717
Phone (716) 271-8960
Phone Toll Free (800) 828-6216
Fax: (800) 828-5539
General preservation supplies, scrapbooks and photo albums.

**7.** University Products, Inc.
P.O. Box 101, Holyoke, MA 01041
Phone (413) 532-3372
Phone Toll Free (800) 628-1912
Fax (800) 532- 9281
General preservation supplies, scrapbooks and photo albums.

**8.** Conservation Support Systems
P.O. Box 91746 Santa Barbara, CA 93190
Phone (805) 682-9843
Phone Toll Free (800) 482-6299
Fax: (805) 682-2064
General preservation supplies.

**9.** Bradley's Plastic Bag Co.
9130 Firestone Blvd. Downey, CA 90241
Phone (213) 923-5556
Phone (818) 289-0811
Phone Toll Free (800) 621-7864
Fax: (310) 862-4474
Plastic supplies of all kinds.

**10.** Archival Products
P.O. Box 1413, Des Moines, IA 50305
Phone Toll Free (800) 247-5323
Fax: (515) 262-6013
General preservation supplies.

**11.** Talas
213 W. 35th St., New York, NY 10001-1996
Phone (212) 219-0770
Fax: (212) 219-0735
General preservation supplies. Specializes in textile supplies.

**12.** Conservation Resources
800-H Forbes Place, Springfield, VA 22151
Phone Toll Free (800) 634-6932
Fax: (703) 321-0629
General preservation supplies.

# APPENDIX

# MAKING COPIES

## *Before a disaster occurs:*

One of the best things you can do to protect yourself if a big disaster hits is to have copies of important documents and family history in a safe place. If you get hit hard enough that you will need to put your life back together, a copy someplace else will really save your bacon. I'm taking about replacement copies for things that you can't afford to loose or that would be a major pain to have to replace. Some of the things that you might want to consider would be:

- ◆ Wills, trust deeds and other estate matters

- ◆ Bank registers

- ◆ Insurance policies

- ◆ Medicaid/Medicare information

- ◆ Passports, green cards

- ◆ Birth certificates

- ◆ Drivers license

- ◆ Family history documents

- ◆ Religious blessings, certificates, declarations

- ◆ Genealogy

- ♦ Irreplaceable certificates and documents that make up your family's history.

- ♦ Anything needed to make an insurance claim.

Your copies need to be kept in a safe dry accessible place... at your mother's house? (or other relative) In a bank vault? At work? A few years ago someone suggested buying a plastic storage container that is sold for arc welding sticks. It seals shut and is water proof. The one I bought is red... a good recognizable color, even in low light, when you're grabbing stuff and heading for the hills. It's a matter of preservation: preserving the information.

### After a disaster occurs:

Let's say you're left with muddy, wet, ripped, ugly piles of important papers. But let us say the information is more important than the original. Give it a rinse if it's wet, dust it off if it's dirty, let it dry and then make photocopies to preserve the information. What's more, the photocopy can be done on acid-free buffered paper (see "Where to Order"). But don't throw away the originals if they are certificates or important documents! Someday, someway, someone will be organized enough and have enough time to get them fixed. Once they are dry, even if they are dirty, wrinkled and ugly, put them in an acid-free buffered box with acid-free buffered interleaving sheets of paper. It would be a good idea to fill out a label with the contents on the outside of the box.

Old, brown, acidic, water stained newspaper articles will cause other things coming into contact with them to deteriorate also. The newspaper itself may be of little interest to you, however the information in the article may want to be kept. A photocopy will be more archival and then put the original newsprint in a folder or sleeve by itself so it does not contaminate anything else. Or perhaps you have ripped, damaged goods. Photocopy it to get a good sturdy copy.

For damaged photos, photographic copywork is done when "restoring" old photographs. The original important photographs should never be touched up by your lo-cal photographer but instead they should make a copy of the photograph and touch up the copy. The final results can be excellent.

This section presents suggestions on how to do your own copy work and will also help you choose the best way to do it, giving you archival standards.

## *Photocopying:*

The photocopy machine will be of great assistance when getting your family history organized and your archives into shape. One of the big benefits of a photocopy ma-chine is that you are able to transfer information onto the kind of paper that you want. Most copy shops have acid-free buffered paper in stock. However, the employees of the store may not know of this paper. Our local Kinko's is a very well furnished, exciting place to do copy work. However, only the owner was able to pull the acid-free paper out of the shelves. May I suggest that you buy a package of 500 sheets of paper (ream) from one of the suppliers in the back of the book and keep this for your photocopying needs.

Photocopying will help to preserve information that looks bad on badly deteriorated papers like newspapers or draw-ings and sketches on butcher paper, etc. In addition, by photocopying letters, sketches, etc. onto paper of a stan-dard size you can take many items of different sizes and copy them onto a standard size sheet and have them bound into a book.

The photocopying process is considered a good, perma-nent archival technique of reproduction by the Library of Congress. The photocopy will be in many ways more per-manent than the original in that the inks will not run when exposed to water and it will not fade when exposed to light. It is important to make sure that there is enough fixer in the photocopy machine and that it will not wipe off onto your hand or smudge after you have made the copies.

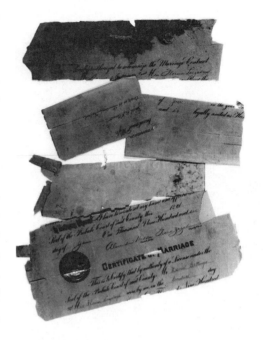

Between September of 1974 and July 1975, my wife and I were getting to know each other through the mail. She was in Italy and I was in the United States. For those eight months or so we corresponded and low and behold years later we both discovered that we saved all of our letters. After chronologically organizing all of her letters, I had them photocopied from the different sized sheets of paper (European sizes differ from American sizes) onto standard 8 1/2" x 11" acid-free buffered sheets and had them bound all together into a book. I then did the same thing to my letters and we were able to solve the question as to who was the most diligent in writing. It was a thrill to be able to flip through the books and read the correspondence and see the development of our relationship.

Another excellent purpose for photocopying is that many halftoning screen built in to the photocopying process. Photocopied photographs were once truly unacceptable, however, now with this new technology many photographs are nicely reproduced and you may find that this is an adequate reproduction of your photographs for other family members or for the use of the same photographic image in different areas of your family history archives.

Another truly amazing development in photocopying technology is the recent quality upgrade of color photocopies. Color photographs, magazine covers, colored drawings, watercolors, etc. can all be reproduced to look almost as nice as the original. If you have already read the section on photography, you will know that color photographs are highly unstable and will not keep their color over the years. The unstable chemicals in the color photography will go out of balance and you will recognize this by some of your old color photographs, which now appear yellow, green, red or blue. The photocopying of photographs will not undergo these alterations and may last much longer then the original photograph. This will depend a lot on the type of paper used and how it is treated. Be aware that it is likely that the colors produced from a color photocopy machine will not age well with daylight. That is, they are likely to fade. The color photocopy will not be affected by water unlike the original color photo. Therefore it will resist future damage better.

One of the most common questions asked about photocopying artwork or important documents is whether or not the photocopying is safe for the artwork and if fading can occur. There are different types of photocopy machines, some which lie on a flat bed and others which suck the document into the machine and spit it back out after the copy is made. It doesn't take too much imagination to foresee the potential damage to an original document if it gets hung up while being sucked up into the machine or if the machine malfunctions in the process. Therefore, I suggest that you only use the type of

Courtesy Conservation Materials, Ltd.

Acid Free Buffered Computer Paper

A recent client came to me with a collection of botanical watercolors, which he wanted to sell. Many attempts to do color photography resulted in poor colors when compared to the original artwork. We were astounded when we saw the quality of the color photocopiers. In fact, when holding up an original watercolor next to the photocopy from three feet away, you could not tell the difference between the copy and the original. He ended up using these copies to send to prospective buyers as well as inventory and catalog records.

machine that has a flat bed. The second part of the question deals with potential fading due to the light and you should not be concerned. The light in the photocopier is intense, however, the short time that the original is exposed to the light is not enough to create any fading problems even if the document were to be photocopied many times.

Another reason for photocopying is that many times you need to present your documents for legal reasons. In the interest of preserving the original document, I suggest that you have copies of the originals made and notarized to be submitted in place of the original. Or for official copies, go to the government office. Federal, state, county and city offices will provide official copies that are as good as originals. Try to avoid handling and sending your originals whenever possible. If you are required to send out originals, try to have them protected in an envelope or encapsulated. Never laminate!

Guidelines for Archival Photocopying
From a report by the Research Libraries Group Preservation Committee

Photocopies whose black ink is well fixed are considered by the Library of Congress to be permanent. Archival quality photocopies require the use of acid-free buffered paper.

**The following are some of the reasons why people make archival copies of important papers:**

♦ Important documents of which you want to have multiple copies in several locations (as a back up in case of disaster)

♦ Family history records (copies for multiple scrapbooks, mailings)

♦ Copying old brittle damaged important papers (protect the original during handling... keep the original safely stored afterwards)

A flat bed scanner...ok to use.

♦

Avoid the copy
machines that suck the
paper inside paper inside.

Or you may find your
important document
chewed up.

♦ Standardizing the size of many irregular sized documents (to be bound?)

♦ Legal needs (never send original irreplaceable documents; have the copy notarized)

♦ Records for insurance companies may include a copy of appraisals and color photocopies of small artwork like watercolors (excellent reproductions are essential in case of a claim).

Copies can be made of photographs (the color photocopier works best or try half toning the original photo prior to copying)

**Follow these steps:**

1. Only black ink photocopies on acid-free buffered paper are considered archival. Color photocopies are not considered archival because they are not permanent. The Library of Congress standard for alkaline reserve is a minimum of 2% by dry weight. This will not be printed on the package but if the company offers an #800 phone number, give them a call and ask. Suitable papers include Xerox XXV Archival Bond, Howard Permalife and University Products Perma-dur. These papers are available through the suppliers listed in this section.

2. There are two types of paper feeders on the copier: 1) the entire surface of the copier moves thereby not changing the position of your original on the glass during the copying or 2) the feeder sucks in the original document and spits it out another slot somewhere else on the machine. Avoid machines with feeder #2. The risk of jamming and damage is too high.

3. Play with the contrast buttons to make sure the copy is as dark as possible without picking up undesirable spots or darkness in the background. Run a test on non archival paper and discard (recycle).

4. Photocopies must be made on a "plain paper" copier. After you have made a copy, try and erase the printed letter: if a freshly made copy smudges, the machine is not fusing the image to the paper properly and the photocopy should not be kept (recycle). Check with the photocopier technician for adjustments.

5. You are photocopying your original page because it needs to be preserved, because it is valuable or because it is deteriorated/damaged. Use extra caution when handling your originals. Carry your items to be copied in protective sleeves and envelopes. Be sure to take extra page protectors for your new photocopies.

6. Only the approved plastics (polyester, polypropylene, polyethylene) will not transfer, or pull the letters off your photocopy onto the plastic. Do not use vinyl or PVC page protectors on anything... even for storing photocopies.

### *Tips on making better photocopies:*

If your original is dirty, yellowed, torn, smudged etc. try the following (get a technician to show you how to work the settings and how to make copies on your acid-free paper):

1. Try making a copy on one of the "light print" settings. It is possible that the blemishes won't show up. This may, however, result in an unsatisfactory light copy, so...

*Make a couple of copies (keep one at another location). Protect it by putting it into a page protector and keep it in a hole book or file.*

2. On regular paper, make the darkest possible copy even though it picks up all the spots and blemishes (without giving an overall grey or dark shadow to the paper).

3. Take the new photocopy (not the original!) and use White Out (or Liquid Paper or something similar) and cover all the imperfections.

4. Make corrections, fill in fractured lines, connect the lines along a tear with a fine tipped pen (black works best) and then...

5. Make a new photocopy. It should be much better than the original now. But if it is not perfect, repeat steps 3 and 4 on the newest photocopy, erasing and adding where needed to make it look right.

6. When you have your perfect copy, then make a final "new original" copy on the acid-free buffered paper (after all your work to make it look good, make a couple of extra copies).

7. Keep the original, "unrestored" old copy safe in the "archives."

Page protectors can be bought to fit 8 1/2" x 11" sheets of paper, with three holes punched for easy storage in notebooks (See "Where to Buy").

### Half-toning:

When a screen is used to give a photograph a dot pattern in order to help it photocopy or print with better clarity, the process is known as half-toning. The process is photographic, however, it should in no way be considered permanent or archival. Within very little time, half-tones can change in shading, intensity and turn yellow. They are, however, excellent for reproducing photographs in newsletters, books, duplication using the photocopying process. If you go to a printer, he will charge a per photograph price, however, many of the copy shops these days have half-toning machines which are much less expensive. For example, a printer may charge you $6-$15 dollars per photograph for half-toning, however, Kinko's will fill an 11" x 17" page with as many photographs as I can fit on it for $10. The half-tone page can then be cut up and used as needed. The results from the half-tone machine will be better then the half-toning screen that is incorporated into the large photocopying machines. Try both to see which is better for your purpose. Usually dark faces and details in shadows will come out better with the half-toning screen on the photocopy machine. Overall, clear photographs will come out better with a real half-tone of the photograph.

The best way to copy a photograph is photographically, however nowadays they are doing some amazing things with scanners and the computer. They can even put your photos on CD Rom disks. Anyway you do it, I suggest making copies of, at least, the most important, "cannot lose" photos.

## *Video Recordings:*

I am often asked about video recording as a means of doing copywork and keeping records. The answer to this question is not simply that I like or do not like this technique. There are several things to consider:

1. Although you can put together a nice presentation of the family and its history, this type of recording is not satisfactorily reproducible in still or print form or other permanent archival uses.

2. Videotapes are a form of magnetic tape, which are not considered to be archival or to have a long life. These tapes will need to be reproduced in the future until a means is discovered to store these moving images on better material.

3. Videotapes are recommended for making a record of all your valuables such as furniture, paintings, books, jewelry, clothing, etc. This type of recording could aid in settling an estate upon death

or should there be a theft or settling with insurance after an emergency situation where a loss has occurred. When recording the details about an item on video, it is important to remember some of the details which help to identify that item.

♦ A title (if artwork) or short accurate description.

♦ Artist or place of manufacturing.

♦ Date when it was made (or a good guess).

♦ Where and when the item was purchased.

♦ How much it cost.

♦ The date of a recent appraisal.

♦ Any important historical information that you have.

♦ If it is a 3 dimensional object, look at the item from many angles and comment on the condition. Incorporating these details into the video tape will make the tape useful in the future.

### *Conclusion:*

Proper copywork will enable you to organize your piles of papers better by helping to standardize their size by reducing them or enlarging them during photocopying (don't throw away the originals). Photocopying with a half-tone can also be an inexpensive means by which you can reproduce photographs for distribution to a number of relatives. Taking photographs of your photographs will give you suitable copies for photo albums and for framing on your ancestor wall (be sure to protect your original photographs dearly). Videotaping is not a good way to keep track of your documents and photographs. However, it is an excellent means of recording a visual family history (including sound, music, etc.), and it is very useful in documenting valuable items in your care in case of emergency situations which involve insurance claims. It is most important to remember never to compromise or damage your originals while making copies.

Do your best to protect them, always keeping them in page protectors. Therefore, it may not be best to feed them into photocopiers that may eat them up, but instead it is better to use machines with flat bed scanners.

A Rarity to missionaries

# Personal Preparation, Emergency Food Storage, Emergency Supplies

Let's say a big enough disaster hits that the stores can't get replenished or maybe the trucks are not getting through. This list suggests what you need to take care of you and your loved ones. Having this stuff stashed away gives a person a very comforting feeling. Consider helping a older person at home alone to get their emergency hoard together too.

In an emergency situation it is possible (if not probable) that the electricity, gas and water will be shut off. Therefore, the foods you store should not require refrigeration or cooking (unless you have a gas BBQ or camping equipment). The quantities suggested are per adult person, for a three day emergency (as you can tell, we're talking survival here... not Club Med). These foods supply 2100 calories daily and essential nutrients.

In an emergency situation it is possible (if not probable) that the electricity, gas and water will be shut off. Therefore, the foods you store should not require refridgeration or cooking (unless you have a gas BBQ or camping equipment).

- ◆ canned tuna fish or pork and beans (1/2 lb/person)

- ◆ nonfat dry milk (1/2 lb/person)

- ◆ graham crackers (1 lb/person)

- ◆ dried apricots (1 lb/person)

- ◆ canned orange or tomato juice (46 oz/person)

- ◆ peanut butter (1/2 lb/person).

- ◆ drinking water 1 gal/person (if you have dehydrated foods stored, you will need more water)

♦ other water (2 gal/person) for food prep., medical needs, hygiene ( 2 1/2 gal supermarket sizes fit well into the hard-to-reach areas of cupboards and under beds)

The above list of essentials may or may not be found today in your cupboards and pantry. Look over what you have and set aside (or hide) these "emergency items" (teenagers can reduce food storage to wrappers in minutes if not well hidden). Throw in a few sweets and family favorites, like candy bars. They will be great for family morale if you are having to live off the stuff on this list.

**Don't forget specialty needs like:**

♦ infant needs (if applicable)

♦ medication

♦ toiletries and personal hygiene

♦ toilet paper (and garbage bags since the toilet won't be working)

♦ first aid supplies (tetanus immunization every five to ten years)

♦ cash

Where will you be during the next disaster? Trouble is you don't know. If it occurs at 4 a.m. like our last earthquake, then you will have many things at home that will make it easier to cope.

But what if it happens while you are at the office? Or out fooling around the countryside on a Saturday. What if roads are blocked off and you can't get home? This happened to me during a huge fire in Santa Barbara when 650 buildings were lost. Have a back up plan. Keep a reserve of emergency items at work (include the needs of your employees), in a storage locker or at a relative or friend's place.

So, let's say you are not home. You would have a hard time opening your can of tuna without a can opener, though I don't doubt that if hungry enough, you would get it open.

A good dry, cool spot for storage is space well used. Look over what you have and set aside these storage items so they don't get used up through normal daily living.

Here's a list of a few things you might find handy:

- can opener

- pan(s) for cooking

- plastic containers for food storage

- dishes and cups (unbreakable)

- eating utensils

- matches (in a waterproof container)

- candles (long lasting emergency candles are best. Scented candles add a nice touch)

- flashlight (don't store the flash light with the batteries inside and have a few extra batteries on hand)

- scriptures

- Teddy Bear, stuffed animals

- ax (for fire wood?)

- shovel

- bucket

- radio (battery powered)

- paper and pencil

- recreational reading material

- trash bags (large and small)

- bedding
    blanket
    cloth sheet
    plastic sheet
    thermal blankets (can be purchased in
        camping supply stores)

- clothing (one change for each person, two pair of socks)

- signal flare

- cleaning supplies

♦ a Boy Scout Handbook

♦ a working bicycle

Many experts think that in a city, by the time three days is up, you should be rescued or assisted by emergency response organizations. In the country this may take longer. The lists of food and supplies are suggested based on this three day period.

Some of the personal documents that you should have copies of, ready to take with you in a protective folder or case include:

♦ family history records, certificates, letters, photographs etc.

♦ genealogical records

♦ religious records

    certificates of baptism
    ordination
    membership
    blessings

♦ appointments

♦ legal documents

    wills
    insurance policies
    contracts (mortgages, loans etc.)
    trust accounts
    passports
    birth certificates
    cars ownership info (contracts, ownership slips, registration etc.)
    ownership records for other major assets

♦ critical medical histories

♦ written permission for medical treatment of minors if guardian or parent is not present

Excellent additional reading:

1. How To Survive An Earthquake (36 pages), See order form in back of this book.
Libby Lafferty CHES of California

2. ESP Earthquake Services and Products Catalog (16 pages incl. price list), 31143 Via Colinas #502, Westlake Village, CA 91362.

The definition of a disaster is an emergency situation for which you were not prepared.

♦ Know where gas shut off valve is located

♦ Know where to shut off electricity

♦ Have an escape route worked out for all family members

♦ Have a place to meet after everyone is out

♦ Practice drills

♦ Buddy system.  Make arrangements to check on someone else and vice versa after an emergency (old folks, single parents with young kids).  Have phone numbers handy.

♦ Learn to use CB radios, short wave radios or other communication methods.

♦ Take a first aid or CPR class (adult ed. at local city college)

# SUGGESTIONS FOR DEALING WITH INSURANCE COMPANIES

If you think the insurance company is your friend, think again. They are a business trying to make money... period. It doesn't matter how well you know your insurance agent either. The company will try to cut corners, find loop holes and avoid paying you, either in part or completely. Now, I'm not trying to be pessimistic. I'm trying to let you see the reality of filing an insurance claim... It ain't gonna be easy to collect your due if it's a big claim. So be well armed... be prepared!

## *Before a disaster occurs:*

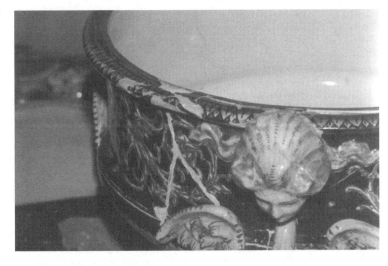

From the family collection of Pope Paul VI

♦ Take pictures of what is insured. For example, a video walk through of the house. Take good care of prints and negatives (see section on photography).

♦ Take detailed pictures of anything that is itemized on the policy. The better the photos, the easier it will be for you to explain your claim later.

♦ Keep a copy of authentication certificates, appraisals, receipts etc. at another location.

♦ Make a copy of the policy and keep it at another location.

A man living six miles from the epicenter of the Northridge Earthquake has over $1 million in china and figurines. But having anchored down everything in his house with Quake Wax, he suffered no damage while all his neighbors had heavy losses. This was the third earthquake he had been through with no damage.

♦ Have an inventory of all your stuff (especially important if you have widespread damage).

♦ Write down the phone numbers of agents, claim offices and keep them in an easy-to-find place (see "Important Phone Numbers List").

♦ Get appraisals or comparison values for anything covered. Update these numbers every once in awhile (5 years?). Remember to get the replacement value." This means that if you had to go out and buy the lost item today from a dealer or store (retail price), what would you have to pay? That's the number you want to give to the insurance company (which may also result in higher premiums).

I've been closely connected with several major disasters (fires in Santa Barbara and Oakland, earthquakes in L.A. and San Francisco) and I have seen how they treat their customers. Also, I have worked as a consultant for insurance companies (fine art claims) and I have worked on numerous restoration projects for them over the last 20 years. What follows is a list of things to remember if you are going to protect yourself.

## *After a Disaster Occurs:*

♦ Take pictures (color prints or video tape will do) of the damaged areas before clean-up starts. If the damage occurred during shipping, take a picture of it broken in the box (before you take it out) and snap a picture of the box too.

♦ Take individual pictures of itemized objects that show damage. Take close-ups of damage.

♦ Contact your insurance agent or the claim's office within the time of the statute of limitations.

♦ Make copies of any papers, documentation and photos that you give to your insurance agent, especially if he is trying to handle an onslaught of claims all at once. Don't give them the original documents.

After you make a claim, the insurance company will determine if you're covered. If you are covered, then they will do two things at their expense:

1. They will have "an expert" evaluate the item to determine the extent and cost of the damage. Often, their expert may be a run-of-the-mill appraiser and not understand the extent or actual costs of damage repair. You are entitled to get another opinion from an expert of your choice. Make sure they will pay for the evaluation before you have it done.

2. They will want to confirm the appraisal or value you have claimed. Again, you have the right to a second opinion. Usually, auction houses and antique stores give lower estimates and specialty galleries give higher estimates.

When considering the damage, the insurance company will want to know from the conservator what damage was "pre-existing" ( the insurance company will not want to pay to clean a picture if it has ripped ). They will only pay for the repair of the damage, IF it does not exceed the value of the object. In other words, they will pay whatever is less: the value of the item or the cost of restoration. You should remember:

♦ Try to find the best conservation professional money can buy. See "Finding a Conservator."

♦ The restoration should bring the condition of the object up to predamaged conditions.

♦ If the value of the object is less because of the damage, even after proper conservation, your insurance company may need to pay you for loss of value.

If your item is a "family heirloom," then it is not in the same category as a "collectible."

♦ Collectibles may require an itemized schedule of insurance or a completely different policy.

♦ A family heirloom should be covered on your homeowner's policy.

♦ The cost of the conservation of a family heirloom should not be based on its value because it cannot be replaced... Therefore, it must be preserved.

I have done the conservation (paid for by insurance companies) on many, many family portraits that were worth $100 - $300 but needed $1000 - $3000 worth of work in order to save them.

# HOW TO FIND A CONSERVATOR

The first place a person usually goes to find a conservator is the yellow pages (under Art Restoration). Some people desire more help in finding qualified professionals and ask museum curators and registrars for a referral. Art galleries and libraries often give out the names of conservators.

There is also a referral system service provided by the national organization for conservation called the The American Institute for Conservation of Historic and Artistic Works (AIC). Referral system information is provided free of charge.

If you would like a referral for a conservator, call or write: The American Institute for Conservation of Historic and Artistic Works (AIC) and FAIC Conservation Services Referral System:

> 1717 K. Street, N.W., Suite 301
> Washington, D.C. 2006
> Tel. (202) 452-9545
> Fax (202) 452-9328

The AIC will give you the names of their members serving your area. Be aware, however, that anyone can join AIC and that membership in AIC does not mean that a person knows what they are doing. AIC does not guarantee the service or quality of the work of its members.

The question should quickly come to mind, "How can I tell a good conservator from a poor one?" "How can I find the best one?"

The following information will give you a few suggestions. I have reproduced for you the brochure, "How to Choose a Conservator" written and published by the American Institute for Conservation of Historic and Artistic Works. (Used with permission)

This brochure will help you select a qualified conservator who can provide sound, ethical preservation services for your art objects, artifacts, and other items of historic and cultural value. The conservation professional can diagnose present and potential problems, provide treatment when necessary, and advise on appropriate conditions for storage and exhibition. The choices you make will directly affect the objects you wish to preserve.

### What is a conservator?

Conservators are concerned with a number of factors in preserving an object, including determining structural stability, counteracting chemical and physical deterioration, and performing conservation treatment based on an evaluation of the aesthetic, historic, and scientific characteristics of the object. Conservation professionals have considerable practical experience, a broad range of theoretical and scientific knowledge, and a commitment to high standards and performance. A conservator may be trained at a conservation graduate training program or by lengthy apprenticeship with experienced senior colleagues. Because of the increasingly technical nature of modern conservation, conservators usually specialize in a particular type of object, such as: paintings, works on paper, textiles, sculpture, furniture, rare books, photographs, or archaeological, decorative, or ethnographic materials. Conservators tend to work in private practice or for a museum, library, historical society, or similar institution.

Sometimes confusion arises about the terms "restoration" and "conservation." Restoration refers to the reconstruction of the aesthetic appearance of an object. Although restoration can be one aspect of conservation, the latter encompasses much more. Conservation involves examination, scientific analysis, and research to determine original structure, materials and extent of loss. Conservation also encompasses structural and environmental treatment to retard future deterioration.

The careful selection of an appropriate conservator is particularly important, because the profession is not regulated by law. The American Institute for Conservation (AIC) is the national organization of conservation professionals. One of its goals is to define and maintain a high level of professionalism in conservation. This goal is reflected in the "AIC Code of Ethics and Standards of Practice," copies of which are available from the AIC office.

FAIC Conservation Services Referral System

The Foundation of the American Institute for Conservation (FAIC) Conservation Services Referral System provides a systematic, consistent method of obtaining current information to identify and locate professional conservation services. The nationwide referral system enables you to address a wide range of conservation problems, whether your needs are long-range or short-term and whether your collection consists of thousands of valuable historic artifacts, one priceless work of art, or items of great personal value. In response to your inquiry, a computer-generated list of conservators is composed and grouped by location, specialization, type of service provided, and AIC membership category (Fellow, Professional Associate or Associate) AIC Professional Associates and Fellows have met specified levels of peer review and have agreed to adhere to the AIC Code of Ethics. Referral system information is provided free of charge.

If you would like a referral for a conservator, call or write: The American Institute for Conservation of Historic and Artistic Works (AIC) and FAIC Conservation Services Referral System:

AIC
1717 K. Street, N.W., Suite 301
Washington, D.C. 2006
Tel. (202) 452-9545
Fax (202) 452-9328

The AIC will give you the names of their members serving your area. Be aware, however, that anyone can join AIC and that membership in AIC does not mean that a person knows what they are doing. AIC does not guarantee the service or quality of the work of its members.

## What Questions to Ask Potential Conservators

Once you have obtained a list of potential conservators from the FAIC Referral System or have compiled one on your own by consulting conservation professionals, conservation organizations, or collectors, you must choose the most appropriate professional. When selecting a conservator to work on your object, seek sufficient information on the individuals under consideration. It may not be appropriate to restrict your search geographically, especially if the object presents unique problems. Many conservators are willing to travel.

**Ask each potential conservator for the following information:**

♦ training

♦ length of professional experience

♦ scope of practice (whether conservation is primary activity)

♦ experience in working with the kind of object for which you seek help

♦ involvement in conservation organizations

♦ availability

♦ references and previous clients

You are making a very important decision. Contact references and previous clients. The quality of conservation work is most accurately evaluated based on the technical and structural aspects of the treatment in addition to the cosmetic appearance; another conservation professional may be able to help you make this evaluation.

For time-consuming projects or collection surveys, you can advertise for a short-term contract conservator in a variety of publications, including the AIC News.

## What to Expect

1. Procedures. A conservator will want to examine the object before suggesting a treatment. Prior to beginning a treatment, the conservator should provide for your review and approval a written preliminary examination report with a description of the proposed treatment, expected results, and estimated cost. The conservator should consult you during the treatment if any serious deviation from the agreed-upon proposal is needed.

2. Cost and Schedule. The conservator should be willing to discuss the basis for all charges. Determine if there are separate rates for preliminary examination and evaluation and if these preliminary charges are separate or deductible from a subsequent contract. Ask questions about insurance, payment terms, shipping, and additional charges. Conservators often have a backlog of work; inquire if a waiting period is necessary before new work can be accepted.

3. Documentation. The conservator should provide a treatment report when treatment is completed. Such reports may vary in length and form but should list materials and procedures used. The final report may, if appropriate, include photographic records documenting condition before and after treatment. Recommendations for

continued care and maintenance may also be provided. Both written and photographic records should be unambiguous. All records should be retained for reference in case the object requires treatment in the future.

**Exercising Caution**

Conservation treatments are frequently time consuming and expensive. Be wary of those who propose to perform a quick and inexpensive restoration job, are reluctant to discuss in detail the materials and methods to be used, or will not permit you to see work in progress. If you have a large collection requiring treatment, you may wish to have one object treated initially before entering into a major contract. The added time or expense of finding the right professional will be small compared to the loss or future costs that could result from inadequate conservation treatment.

It is also important to note that conservators do not always agree. Ask about risks involved with certain treatment options. Speak to a number of conservators if you are unable to make a comfortable decision.

**Points to Remember when Selecting a Conservator**

♦ Learn about the field of conservation

♦ Seek advice and recommendations through the FAIC Conservation Service Referral System and other professional organizations.

♦ Contact a conservator's previous clients. Investigate references.

♦ Request information regarding the conservator's background, training, experience, and professional affiliation.

♦ Expect to receive the following from a professional conservator:

1. Written preliminary examination report evaluating condition, proposing treatment, describing limitations of treatment, and providing an estimate of the treatment cost and duration.

2. Notification during treatment of major changes in the proposal.

3. Written and, if appropriate, photographic documentation of the treatment.

## Information Sources

The American Institute for Conservation of Historic and Artistic Works (AIC) 1400 16th Street, N.W., Suite 340, Washington, DC 20036 Tel.: (202) 232-6636, Fax: (202) 232-6630

AIC is the national organization of conservation professionals which sponsors conferences and publishes and sells a variety of conservation-related periodicals. Its nonprofit foundation, The Foundation of the American Institute for Conservation of Historic and Artistic Works (FAIC), offers educational programs, grants to conservators, and the referral system. A general bibliography on conservation is available on request.

National Institute for the Conservation of Cultural Property (NIC), 3299 K Street, N.W, Suite 403, Washington, DC 20007
Tel.: (202) 625-1495, Fax: (202) 625-1485

NIC provides a forum for discussion, understanding, and awareness of national conservation and preservation needs. NIC offers bibliographies and other publications on a wide range of conservation and related topics.

Getty Conservation Institute (GCI),
4503 Glencoe Avenue, Marina del Rey, CA 90292
Tel.: (213) 822-2299, Fax: (213) 821-9409

GCI addresses conservation problems on cultural property through its programs in scientific research, training, documentation, and publications and its administration of the Conservation Information Network (CIN).

The International Institute for Conservation of Historic and Artistic Works (IIC),
6 Buckingham Street, London, England  WC2N 6BA
Tel.: 01-1441-839-5975

IIC-CG (Canadian Group), P. O. Box 9195,
Terminal, Ottawa, Ontario  K1G 3T9, Canada
Tel.:  (613) 998-3721, Fax:  (613) 998-4721

IIC and IIC-CG are two of the international organizations dedicated to conservation that produce publications and organize professional meetings.

Regional Conservation Organizations or Guilds Regional and Local conservation associations provide a forum for information exchange among conservators.  Their meetings are open to anyone interested in conservation.  The AIC national office can provide the address of the regional organization in your geological area.

If you need assistance or further information, please contact the AIC national office.

# A List of Good Books

### Good Books to Read on Photographic Needs

* *Collection, Use and Care of Historical Photographs* , by Weinstein and Booth, published by the American Association for State and Local History (AASLH) 1400 Eighth Ave. South, Nashville, Tennessee, 37203

* *Care and Identification of 19th Century Photographic Prints* , by James Reilly published by Eastman Kodak Co., Dept. 412L, 343 State St., Rochester, NY, 14650-0532

* *Conservation of Photographs*, published by Eastman Kodak Co., Dept. 412L, 343 State St., Rochester, NY, 14650-0532

### Good books to read on a Variety of Materials, Fine Art, Furniture, Textiles, & Objects

* *Handle with Care:  Preserving Your Heirlooms*, by Davis, Nancy.  1991 (31 p.).: Rochester Museum and Science Center, Research Division, 657 East Ave., Box 1480, Rochester, NY 14603-1480.  (716) 271-4320.

* *Way to Go! Crating Artwork for Travel*,  1985 (53 p.), Gallery Association of New York State, Inc., P.O. Box 345, Hamilton, NY 13346. (315) 824-2510.

### Good books to read on Books and Paper

* *The Care of Prints and Drawings*, by Ellis, Margaret H., 1987 (264 p.)  The American Association for State and Local History, 530 Church St., 6th Fl., Nashville, TN 37219-2325. (615) 255-2971.

* *The Care of Fine Books*, by Greenfield, Jane, Nick Lyons Books, 1988 (224 p.)  Distributed by Lyons and Burford, 31 W. 21st St., New York, NY 10010. (212) 620-9580.

* *How to Care for Works of Art on Paper* ; 4th ed., by Perkinson, Roy L. and Francis W. Dolloff, 1985 (48 p.) Museum of Fine Arts, Gift Shop, 465 Huntington Ave., Boston, MA 02115. (617) 267-9300.

* *Matting and Hinging of Works of Art on Paper*, by Smith, Merrily A. (compiler), Washington, DC: Library of Congress, 1981 (31 p.) Distributed by Conservation of Art on Paper, 2805 Mt. Vernon Ave., Ste. B, Alexandria, VA 22301. (703) 836-7757.

### Good books to read on Glass, Paintings and Textiles

* *China Mending: A Guide to Repairing and Restoration.* by Evetts, Echo, 1983 (155 p.) Faber and Faber, Inc., 50 Cross St., Winchester, MA 01890. (617) 721-1427.

* *The Care of Pictures,* by Stout, George, 1975 (176 p.) Dover Publications, 31 E. Second St., Mineola, NY 11501. (516) 294-7000.

* *Considerations for the Care of Textiles and Costumes: A Handbook for the Non-Specialist.* 1980 (24 p.) Indianapolis Museum of Art, Catalogue Sales, 1200 W. 38th St., Indianapolis, IN, 46208. (317) 923-1331.

### The NET

If you would like to read conservation information on **Internet**, Stanford University, a Project of the Preservation Dept. of SU Libraries is currently sponsoring "Conservation OnLine" (CoOL). Address: cool-cfl.src.stanford.edu

### Other Good Books

* *How To Survive An Earthquake* (36 pages), Libby Lafferty CHES of California. Order from Preservation Help Publications, $5 (incl. tax and s/h) P.O. Box 1206, Santa Barbara, CA 93102, 1 (800) 833-9226

* *ESP Earthquake Services and Products Catalog* (16 pages incl. price list), 31143 Via Colinas #502, Westlake Village, CA 91362

# INDEX

# ABOUT THE AUTHOR

Scott M. Haskins (born in Los Angeles, 1953) has been working in the conservation field since 1975. For several years he studied and lived in Lombardy, Italy (Brescia, Garda Lake area). In 1979, he set up and ran the conservation laboratory at Brigham Young University in Provo, Utah where he also serviced the historical art collection of the Church of Jesus Christ of Latter-Day Saints. In 1984, he moved his family back to Southern California to settle in Santa Barbara.

Mr. Haskins' conservation business, Fine Art Conservation Laboratories (FACL, Inc.) specializes in the conservation of paintings on canvas, panels, paper and on walls in historic buildings (murals). FACL provides painting conservation services to the general public, collectors, dealers, auction houses, museums, institutions with art holdings and to city, state and federal governments throughout the United States. Some of his more visible clients have included Holland America Lines, Hearst Castle, The City of Los Angeles, The Mission Inn, The Friends of Mexico Foundation, The Church of Jesus Christ of Latter-Day Saints, the Archdiocese of Los Angeles, Pope Paul's family collection, The International Institute of Iberian Art and The Santa Barbara Museum of Art.

His interest in family history and genealogy prompted his activities in genealogical research while living in Italy and in the United States. Because of his background in preservation, he is often approached by people with boxes of photos and certificates that need help.

Mr. Haskins has been an active speaker and lecturer over the years at professional conferences throughout the USA, in Canada, France and Italy. He is often invited as a guest speaker at historical conferences and seminars.

In 1989, Scott accepted the chance to teach an adult education class at Santa Barbara City College on the Preservation of Treasured Family Documents. The teaching experience, for the last 7 years, has given Mr. Haskins the chance to refine his approach to the public and translate the technical publications into easily understood step by step instructions which are so characteristic of his 'how-to' teaching techniques.

"How To Save Your Stuff From A Disaster, complete instructions on how to protect and save your family history, heirlooms and collectibles" is Mr. Haskins' first book.

# How To Save Your Stuff From A Disaster

### *by Scott Haskins*

## Order Form

\* Fax Orders:  (805) 568 1178
\* Telephone Orders:  1 (800) 833 9226
\* Postal orders:  Preservation Help Publishing, P. O. Box 1206, Santa Barbara, CA
    93102,  USA  (805) 899 9226

I am enclosing $19.95 for each book, plus                              _____
Shipping & Handling $4.95 for 1st book + $.75 for each additional book     _____
Tax        7.75% in California                                        _____
                                               Total     _____

Payment:

\_\_\_\_\_ Check
\_\_\_\_\_ Credit Card:  \_\_\_\_\_Visa  \_\_\_\_\_ Mastercard  Credit Card #  _____

Name on card_____Exp. Date _____

Please send my order to:

Name_____
Company_____
Address_____
City_____State_____Zip_____
Telephone (          )_____

"As a self-help book it is the ultimate manual... This is a must have for anyone who prizes the family's photo, papers, etc... even without a home disaster."

Juanita Thinnes, Past President, Friends of the Historic Mission Inn, Riverside, CA and genealogist.

## *"Give this page to a friend or family member"*

# How To Save Your Stuff From A Disaster

## *by Scott Haskins*

## Order Form

* Fax Orders:  (805) 568 1178
* Telephone Orders:  1 (800) 833 9226
* Postal orders:  Preservation Help Publishing, P. O. Box 1206, Santa Barbara, CA
  93102,  USA  (805) 899 9226

I am enclosing $19.95 for each book, plus                          _____

Shipping & Handling $4.95 for 1st book + $.75 for each additional book          _____

Tax          7.75% in California                          _____

Total          _____

Payment:

_____ Check

_____ Credit Card:  \_\_\_\_\_Visa \_\_\_\_\_ Mastercard  Credit Card #  _____

Name on card_____Exp. Date _____

Please send my order to:

Name_____

Company_____

Address_____

City_____State_____Zip_____

Telephone (          )_____

"As a self-help book it is the ultimate manual... This is a must have for anyone who prizes the family's photo, papers, etc... even without a home disaster."

Juanita Thinnes, Past President, Friends of the Historic Mission Inn, Riverside, CA and genealogist.

## *"Give this page to a friend or family member"*

# How To Save Your Stuff From A Disaster

### *by Scott Haskins*

## Order Form

* Fax Orders:  (805) 568 1178
* Telephone Orders:  1 (800) 833 9226
* Postal orders:  Preservation Help Publishing, P. O. Box 1206, Santa Barbara, CA
  93102,  USA  (805) 899 9226

I am enclosing $19.95 for each book, plus                                    _____

Shipping & Handling $4.95 for 1st book + $.75 for each additional book      _____

Tax          7.75% in California                                            _____

Total      _____

Payment:

_____ Check

_____ Credit Card:  _____Visa  _____ Mastercard  Credit Card #  _____

Name on card_____Exp. Date _____

Please send my order to:

Name_____

Company_____

Address_____

City_____State_____Zip_____

Telephone (          )_____

"As a self-help book it is the ultimate manual... This is a must have for anyone who prizes the family's photo, papers, etc... even without a home disaster."

Juanita Thinnes, Past President, Friends of the Historic Mission Inn, Riverside, CA and genealogist.

## *"Give this page to a friend or family member"*

# How To Survive An Earthquake
### by
### Libby Lafferty
### Ches of California

## Order Form

\* Fax Orders:  (805) 568 1178
\* Telephone Orders:  1 (800) 833 9226
\* Postal orders:  Preservation Help Publishing, P. O. Box 1206, Santa Barbara, CA
  93102,  USA  (805) 899 9226

Please send me _____ copies of How To Survive An Earthquake (36 pages).
I understand that I may return my order for a full refund, No questions asked.

I am enclosing $5.00 for each book                                            _____
(We will pay the shipping and taxes if applicable)
                                                    Total          _____

Payment:

_____ Check
_____ Credit Card:  _____Visa _____  Mastercard  Credit Card #  _____

Name on card_____ Exp. Date_____

Please send my order to:

Name_____
Company_____
Address_____
City_____State_____Zip_____
Telephone (          )_____

"This book is packed with 36 pages of precise, easy to follow instructions.  It is the best
I've seen on the subject.  It is very helpful.
Scott M. Haskins, author of "How To Save Your Stuff From A Disaster"

## *Please inquire about quantity discounts.*

# How To Survive An Earthquake
by
**Libby Lafferty**
**Ches of California**

# Order Form

* Fax Orders:  (805) 568 1178
* Telephone Orders:  1 (800) 833 9226
* Postal orders:  Preservation Help Publishing, P. O. Box 1206, Santa Barbara, CA
   93102,  USA  (805) 899 9226

Please send me _____ copies of How To Survive An Earthquake (36 pages).
I understand that I may return my order for a full refund, No questions asked.

I am enclosing $5.00 for each book                                    _____
(We will pay the shipping and taxes if applicable)
                                                        Total          _____

Payment:

_____ Check
_____ Credit Card:  _____Visa  _____  Mastercard  Credit Card # _____

Name on card_____ Exp. Date_____

Please send my order to:

Name_____
Company_____
Address_____
City_____State_____Zip_____
Telephone (          )_____

"This book is packed with 36 pages of precise, easy to follow instructions.  It is the best
I've seen on the subject.  It is <u>very</u> helpful.
Scott M. Haskins, author of "How To Save Your Stuff From A Disaster"

*Please inquire about quantity discounts.*

# How To Survive An Earthquake
**by**
**Libby Lafferty**
**Ches of California**

# Order Form

\* Fax Orders:  (805) 568 1178
\* Telephone Orders:  1 (800) 833 9226
\* Postal orders:  Preservation Help Publishing, P. O. Box 1206, Santa Barbara, CA
  93102,  USA  (805) 899 9226

Please send me _____ copies of How To Survive An Earthquake (36 pages).
I understand that I may return my order for a full refund, No questions asked.

I am enclosing $5.00 for each book                              _____
(We will pay the shipping and taxes if applicable)
                                    Total              _____


Payment:

_____ Check
_____ Credit Card:  \_\_\_\_\_Visa \_\_\_\_\_  Mastercard  Credit Card #  _____

Name on card_____ Exp. Date_____

Please send my order to:

Name_____
Company_____
Address_____
City_____State_____Zip_____
Telephone (          )_____

"This book is packed with 36 pages of precise, easy to follow instructions.  It is the best
I've seen on the subject.  It is very helpful.
Scott M. Haskins, author of "How To Save Your Stuff From A Disaster"

## *Please inquire about quantity discounts.*